Here Come the
Bride Dolls

For Michael and our little best man, Harrison.

CR BO

First edition/First printing

To purchase additional copies of this book, please contact:
Portfolio Press, 130 Wineow Street, Cumberland, MD 21502
877-737-1200

Library of Congress Control Number 2001-130308
ISBN 0-942620-49-6

Project Editor: Krystyna Poray Goddu
Design and Production: Tammy S. Blank
Cover design by John Vanden-Heuvel Design
Cover photo: Tyler Wentworth Bride by Robert Tonner
Cover photo by Storm Photo/Courtesy Robert Tonner Doll Company
Back cover: To Have and To Hold by Stephanie Blythe
Back cover photo by Jerry Anthony/Courtesy Stephanie Blythe

Printed and bound in Korea

Here Come the

Bride Dolls

Louise Fecher

Portfolio Press

Contents

Introduction

A timeless and evocative symbol of love and beauty, a bride is so much more than a woman dressed for her wedding day. She is the brightest star—the beacon on which all eyes happily rest—at the most joyful cultural, social, and religious event celebrated throughout the world. As she walks gracefully down the aisle to meet her chosen partner for life, a bride reminds us of the most precious gifts that one human being can offer another: an open heart, a trusting soul, and a hopeful spirit.

Given the universal appeal of the bride and the smiles and sighs that she elicits in all who view her, it's no surprise that her image has been captured by painters and photographers, her praises sung by poets and philosophers. Dollmakers, too, be they large manufacturers, cottage industries, or an individual artist working in a cozy home studio, have found in the bride an irresistible image. As a doll, the bride has been interpreted in countless ways: as a medieval maiden, as a saucy Roaring Twenties flapper, as an imaginary princess who weds in a fantasy realm. Some dollmakers have recreated famous brides from history; others have been inspired by legends, myths, and other works of fiction. But for most dollmakers, especially those who have revisited the wedding theme again and again, the bride is the lovely lady in white, a radiant vision of romance.

In this book, the reader will find more than one hundred of the best-loved and most notable bride dolls produced by artists, manufacturers, and designers from the mid-1980s through 2000. Most of the dolls shown are no longer made; many are highly coveted limited editions or one-of-a-kind works of art. Some sold for under a hundred dollars when introduced; others, particularly the one-of-a-kind dolls, had impressive four-figure price tags.

As a wedding gift, of sorts, to readers of *Here Come the Bride Dolls*, I invited a number of dollmakers to create one-of-a-kind or limited-edition pieces exclusively for debut in this book. These never-before-seen dolls are sprinkled throughout the book, like jewels in a bridal tiara. Within this book I have also included a number of vintage and contemporary wedding photographs. Some depict famous brides and are shown alongside the dolls that they inspired. Other photos were generously contributed by family, friends, and associates. Like the dolls with which they are shown, these delightful images offer glimpses of wedding fashions and trends. In several cases, a gown worn by a real-life bride or bridesmaid even bears an uncanny—and

Bernice and Walter Fecher (the author's parents), April 18, 1953

coincidental—resemblance to a dress worn by a doll. Most important, these photos—fresh from the donors' wedding albums—remind us that our mementos, be they photos, dolls, or dried and pressed petals from a bridal bouquet, will keep our memories fresh for a lifetime.

Something Old . . .

Each year at the American International Toy Fair in New York City, where new dolls are shown to prospective buyers from around the world, a procession of new brides make their debut. A perpetually popular seller, the bride is an enduring theme for many dollmakers. The Alexander Doll Company, the New York City-based manufacturer founded in 1923 by the indomitable and innovative Beatrice Alexander, offered its first bride (a seven-inch composition doll) in the 1930s. But it was in the postwar years, the late 1940s through the mid 1950s (a time when both real-life brides and doll-size ones proliferated), when the company created its "really magnificent examples," says Lia Sargent, a dealer, collector, and well-known authority on Madame Alexander dolls made prior to 1965.

The most coveted Alexander bride from this era is the 21-inch hard-plastic *Deborah Bride* of 1951, who wears a sumptuous Victorian ensemble of ivory satin. (An extremely rare doll, she sells for $15,000 in mint condition, Lia Sargent says.) Other pop-

Above: A vintage 1961 Barbie modeling "Wedding Day Set," the first wedding ensemble produced by Mattel for the formidable fashion doll
Right: the 1950 Bride (left) and the Lucy Bride from 1948, both 21 inches
Below: The Alexander Doll Company's Pink Bride of 1950

ular early Madame Alexander brides include the 21-inch *Lucy Bride* of 1948, who wears a satin gown with a rhinestone-studded bodice; the 21-inch *Pink Bride* of 1950, who is garbed in blush-pink satin accented with net; and the 21-inch *1950 Bride*, who's dressed similarly to the *Pink Bride*, but in white rayon and lace. (According to Lia Sargent, mint examples of these brides bring $1,650, $1,800, and $1,500, respectively.)

Through the years, the Alexander Doll Company has continued to recreate the bride in all her glory, wearing eye-catching confections that reflect the prevailing fashions of the day. Bride dolls are so popular, notes Daun Fallon, Alexander's vice president of design, that the company includes a minimum of three brides in its line every year.

Mattel, the maker of Barbie, produced its first bridal costume for the formidable fashion doll in 1959, the same year that Barbie was born. "It was called 'Wedding Day Set,' and it was available from 1959 to 1962. At the time it was the most expensive outfit for Barbie: it was five dollars," says A. Glenn Mandeville, a noted doll and toy author, collector, and historian. (Today, a mint-in-package example of this satin and tulle ensemble fetches $500 and up.) "Wedding Day Set" was followed by other wedding ensembles for Barbie (the highly coveted "Beautiful Bride" outfit from 1967 can fetch as much as

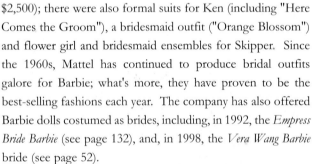

Left: Yvonne, circa 1870s French bisque-headed fashion doll, 25 inches, wears a handmade bridal gown.
Above: Mrs. Raffaela Celentano Palmiere in miniature: the gown worn by this 20-inch hard-plastic doll is an exact copy of the real one, shown on the opposite page.

$2,500); there were also formal suits for Ken (including "Here Comes the Groom"), a bridesmaid outfit ("Orange Blossom") and flower girl and bridesmaid ensembles for Skipper. Since the 1960s, Mattel has continued to produce bridal outfits galore for Barbie; what's more, they have proven to be the best-selling fashions each year. The company has also offered Barbie dolls costumed as brides, including, in 1992, the *Empress Bride Barbie* (see page 132), and, in 1998, the *Vera Wang Barbie* bride (see page 52).

Doll collectors have not always had a bevy of ready-made bridal beauties to choose from, however. The antique bride dolls that exist today, whether in private or public collections, were probably not dressed as brides by the companies that manufactured them. Rather, experts believe, the dolls were dressed as brides by their owners (not necessarily the original owners)—possibly as mementos of real-life weddings.

The Brides of New York

The Toy Collection at the Museum of the City of New York in Upper Manhattan counts among its residents a number of heirloom bride dolls once owned by that city's wealthy founding families. When the museum was established in the 1920s, many of the descendants of New York City's elite were leaving their mansions for smaller homes and, consequently, were looking to dispose of many of their possessions. Many of these treasures, including dolls, were donated to the museum,

explains John Darcy Noble, former curator of the museum's Toy Collection and a respected and well-loved authority on dolls, in the January 1994 issue of *Dolls* magazine. In his article, he talks about the bride *Yvonne*, a 25-inch bisque-headed French fashion doll, dated circa 1870s. She is a "very expensive and superior creature," says Mr. Noble, who goes on to describe her gown:

> *The fabric used is a very costly corded silk, ivory-colored. There is an overdress with princess lines, and it is gathered on the right-hand side to the knee over an embroidered lace. The asymmetrical closure, from the right shoulder to the left hip, is trimmed with the same embroidered lace and punctuated with posies of orange blossoms.*

Mr. Noble suggests that *Yvonne*'s "grand garment" was made as a replica of a bride's dress, using actual remnants from that dress, by a professional dressmaker. "We have no evidence that this is the case here, but the immense assurance of this dress suggests that this was so," he concludes.

One of the loveliest bride dolls at the Museum of the City of New York is of more recent vintage. In this case, we need not speculate on her origins. The doll was donated by her owner, Raffaela Celentano Palmiere, and wears an exact copy of Mrs. Palmiere's breathtaking handmade bridal gown of 1948. Both the full-size garment and the miniature one were painstakingly crafted by retired dressmaker Stella Saracino. "She was a little Italian lady from the Bronx, and she made the most gorgeous

Raffaela Celentano Palmiere in her splendid handmade wedding gown of 1948

Below: Mary Lewis's china Charlie Gilmore ring bearer, circa 1865, 12½ inches, shown with a German bride and groom, circa 1880
Right: Dorothy Heizer's Princess Elizabeth wedding portrait doll, about 15 inches, 1948

gowns you ever saw in your life," says Mrs. Palmiere, who remembers her own bridal gown with pleasure. "It was made of 'slipper satin,' as they called it at the time," she says, "and it was inspired by one of the costumes that Sonja Henie wore." The full, long-trained skirt "looked like a checker board," she adds, with squares of pleated silk satin alternating with squares decorated with sequins, bugle beads, and pearls stitched in the shape of a plume.

Mrs. Palmiere's bride doll was made about a year after her marriage, as a keepsake. An unmarked, 20-inch hard-plastic doll was used as the model. "She was absolutely magnificent," Mrs. Palmiere says of the exquisitely costumed doll, which enjoyed a place of honor in her home. "I kept her encased in glass in my bedroom, on a gold-leaf table." When Mrs. Palmiere moved to a smaller home, she decided, with more than a little sadness, to donate her beloved doll to the museum. "I cried when I gave her up, but now the whole world can enjoy her," she says. "The museum will be there forever; they will take care of her," she adds. (Mrs. Palmiere's gown will also be preserved for posterity; it's in the collection of the Costume Institute of New York City's Metropolitan Museum of Art.)

Born in New York City in the late 1890s, Mary E. Lewis was a pioneer among doll collectors. In 1937, she founded the National Doll & Toy Collectors Club, the precursor of the United Federation of Doll Clubs (UFDC), the international organization for doll collectors. "Mary collected all kinds of dolls, but she was especially intrigued with brides," recalls Barbara Steiker, a well-known proponent of doll collecting. In the mid 1940s, Mary Lewis helped research and organize an exhibit of dolls that traced the history of wedding traditions. Called "A Gallery of Diamonds and Dolls," the exhibit showcased dolls alongside diamond engagement rings, and was shown in jewelry stores across the United States. (Each doll in the exhibit also had its own custom-made jewelry, made with real gold and diamonds!) The exhibit was the subject of a book, *The Marriage of Diamonds and Dolls* (H.L. Lindquist Publications, New York), written in 1947 by Mary E. Lewis and Dorothy Dignam, her collaborator on the exhibit. In the book, Mrs. Lewis talks about her very first bride doll:

Mr. Lewis and I never had a daughter of our own so I had no one to wear my own wedding finery. One day I came across an old box with all my outfit in it—dress, slippers, veil, gloves and underwear. I wanted more

Princess Elizabeth, future Queen of England, and Philip Mountbatten, Duke of Edinburgh, on their November 20, 1947 wedding day

room in the attic to store my dolls so the thought came to me, "Why not have a bride doll dressed out of my wedding things?" So I shook out the tissue paper and looked up my old wedding pictures and had this doll costumed just as I had been with the same kind of jewelry and flowers. I had her little white kid gloves made from mine and her little shoes from the scraps that were left.

The *Little Mrs. Lewis* bride—a 26-inch antique German bisque and composition doll—was costumed by Lulu Kriger in charmeuse satin taken from Mary Lewis's gown. Mrs. Lewis also had Lulu Kriger dress many of her antique porcelain, china, and wax dolls as brides and wedding party members. Her 12½-inch *Charlie Gilmore* ring bearer, a rare china boy dated circa 1865, is now in the collection of the Strong Museum in Rochester, New

York. He is handsomely outfitted in an embroidered silk shirt and a black velvet suit. Even more impressive than his attire, however, are the tiny rings he dutifully carries, which are stitched onto a satin cushion. In *The Marriage of Diamonds and Dolls*, Mary Lewis writes: "They are smaller than peas. One is an engagement ring with a real diamond weighing only 1/100 of a carat, set in gold prongs just like a full-size ring, and the other is a tiny wedding band to match."

The most precious jewel in Mary Lewis's collection was a stunning portrait of Princess Elizabeth as a bride, created in 1948 by Dorothy Heizer, a brilliant artist whose works are held in the highest esteem today. Dorothy Heizer was a charter member of the prestigious National Institute of American Doll

Artists (now known as NIADA), founded in 1962 by artist and author Helen Bullard with help from artists Gertrude Florian, Fawn Zeller, and Magge Head. Like all of Dorothy Heizer's works, *Princess Elizabeth* is a sculpture in fabric. Built on a wire foundation, the doll is constructed of layers of cotton eiderdown covered with a cotton crepe "skin." Her face—a striking likeness of the young woman who would be queen—was carefully modeled in fabric and handpainted by the artist, who referred to photographs of the princess as she worked.

A 1949 program for the Diamonds and Dolls exhibit describes *Princess Elizabeth*'s ensemble as "almost beyond belief in beauty and exquisite detail." Made of slipper satin with a chiffon train, the miniature bridal gown is adorned with over 44,000 seed pearls and rhinestones, arranged in the same exact pattern as in the princess's royal gown of 1947. The doll also wears a platinum crown with a tulle veil and pearl jewelry. On her finger, *Princess Elizabeth* wears the smallest engagement ring in the world. According to a 1977 article in *New York-Pennsylvania Collector* written by former Strong Museum curator Margaret

Whitton, the ring is 14-karat gold with a .11 carat diamond, and was made by the Artcarved company at the request of Mary Lewis. An awe-inspiring work of art, *Princess Elizabeth* is part of the collection at the Strong Museum. (Despite the intense labor that went into the making of this doll, Heizer accepted eight more commissions for *Princess Elizabeth* brides.)

Dorothy Heizer was not the only early doll artist who created brides; Helen Bullard, Halle Blakeley, Martha Thompson, and many others created their own variations on the theme. The most prolific maker of bride dolls was Ada Odenrider, who was accepted into NIADA in 1969. Ada Odenrider chronicled the history of bridal fashions from 1800 to 1969 with a spectacular series of forty-five dolls. Made of porcelain or china and costumed by the artist, the dolls were displayed at the Seattle Museum of History and Industry in 1978 in conjunction with the UFDC's convention that year. They were also the subject of the artist's self-published book, *Wedding Belles of Dolls and Costumes.*

Martha Thompson's portrait of Princess Grace of Monaco in her bridal attire, porcelain and cloth, about 21 inches, 1957

The October 4, 1958, wedding party of Anna and George Petro (the author's in-laws)

Something New . . .

Among the most prolific makers of brides today are the British duo Paul Crees and Peter Coe, whose stunning version of Princess Diana appears on pages 102 and 103. "We find bride dolls so appealing as it is such a romantic theme," says Paul Crees. "There's no better theme for a designer," Peter Coe adds. "You have centuries of changing fashions and styles to inspire you."

Artist/designer Robert Tonner, who created the lovely bride who graces this book's cover, made his first bride doll in 1995 (see page 60). "Having grown up in the 1950s, I remember the bride dolls of those days: They were the cream of the crop. I want to bring back that magic: a beautiful wedding gown on a beautiful doll," he says.

A modern-day Mary Lewis, North Carolina collector Phyllis West owns many vintage and contemporary bride dolls made by the makers featured in this book. Like Mary Lewis, she collects many kinds of dolls, but the brides are by far her favorites. "They are the ones my heart goes to," she says. "When I see a bride, I think about the inner joy she's feeling. The gowns are so varied, yet the dream that the bride represents—a wonderful dream—is always the same."

Like Raffaela Palmiere, many brides commemorate their wedding with a keepsake doll, even if they are not collectors. Seamstresses are often willing to make replicas of gowns on generic hard-plastic dolls or fashion dolls like Barbie. Ambitious brides may choose to sew a doll costume

themselves. (To commemorate her marriage to George Petro on October 4, 1958, my mother-in-law, Anna Petro, costumed nine dolls: a bride for herself, plus one doll for each member of her bridal party!)

When I was married in 1996, I dressed dolls from my own collection to represent my wedding party. A 1970 "Living Barbie" and a 1991 male fashion doll from Mattel ("Brandon

The author and her husband, Michael Petro, celebrate their October 20, 1996, wedding with Barbie and her groom.

Above left: This unique keepsake bride, resin and fabric, 18 inches, was created by French artist Héloïse as a wedding gift in 2000. Above right: Sheila Wallace McKay's Memory Angel, 13 inches, clay and fabric, is dressed in fabrics and trims from a vintage wedding gown.

Walsh" from the licensed *Beverly Hills 90210* doll series) stood in as bride and groom. The bride wore the gown and veil from the "Bride's Dream" Barbie ensemble (1963-65); the groom wore a Mattel "Fashion Avenue" tuxedo produced in the 1990s. Gigi Williams, owner of the shop Gigi's Dolls & Sherry's Teddy Bears in Chicago, received a spectacular keepsake for her June 2000 wedding: the French artist Héloïse, a longtime friend, presented her with a custom-made doll dressed in vintage lace. A number of brides have commissioned artist Sheila Wallace McKay to make their wedding-day keepsakes. The artist, who for years specialized in making historical costume dolls, began offering custom-made *Memory Angels* in the late 1990s. Made of clay, they are costumed in bits of fabric and trim taken from the bride's wedding dress.

Of course, most bride dolls will not end up in a museum or be worth thousands of dollars! Whether plastic or china, homemade or artist-made, exquisitely dressed in satin or simply draped in a bit of ribbon, what makes them special is the memories and dreams that they represent. As I worked on this book, I found myself reminiscing about my wedding. But, even more important, I often thought back to when I was a young girl in the 1970s, fantasizing about weddings and romance: Would I ever be married? Would I be a beautiful bride? Would I change my name, or stick to my guns and keep the one I was born with?

Long-forgotten memories awoke, and I vividly remembered looking through issues of *Bride's* and other magazines and clipping the pictures of my favorite gowns. I'm sure that millions of other young girls did—and still do—the same, and it is my hope that this book sparks the imagination of the reader in the same way that the bride magazines did for me years ago. Let this book be, for you, a portfolio of dreams, and go where the vision takes you.

Medieval Maidens and Victorian Visions

White was worn by brides of the ancient world (in Egypt and Greece), but it was not *de rigeuer* for European and American brides until the nineteenth century, when two famous brides—Mary Hellen, who wed the son of President John Quincy Adams in 1828, and Queen Victoria, who married Prince Albert in 1840—donned white satin to take their vows. One of the earliest white wedding gowns recorded in Europe dates from the 1490s. The bride was Anne of Brittany; the groom, Louis XII. This was an exception, not the rule: in fifteenth-century Europe, white was not a popular color for brides.

"Fashions of the mid-fifteenth century dictated rich, dark colors, the most popular being gold, red, blue, and green accented with white, black, or a dark contrasting color," says Charles Batte, the creator of *Lady Anne*, a medieval bride. A noblewoman, she is splendidly outfitted for her wedding in her best and most fashionable gown, which, notes Batte, "would be worn later for grand occasions." (Even nineteenth-century brides wore their wedding gowns after the marriage.) Made of gold silk brocade, the gown has a plunging neckline with an inset of metallic silk chiffon, and a high waistline girded by a pearl-studded metallic belt. The gown's collar and cuffs are iridescent burgundy velvet (during this period, the cuffs covered the hands); this same velvet trims the hem. The dress has *two* long trains: one in front and one in back. "Walking in such a gown required great care," Batte points out. He describes the technique: "The lady would gather the front train over one arm, lean to the side, and gently push the back train to the side as she gracefully turned in wide circles."

Lady Anne's conical headdress, or hennin, is made of antique silk brocade trimmed with gold braid, ruby crystals, and faux pearls. It sits far back on the head, secured by a small, velvet-covered wire loop over the forehead. The hennin concealed the hair, and fashionable ladies even shaved or plucked their hairlines, creating the look of a high forehead. The bride's hennin is covered with a white silk organza veil edged with gold thread. The veil's pink hue is due to artful lighting, which lets us imagine that the bride stands in a ray of sunlight streaming through a stained glass window.

Created especially for debut in *Here Come the Bride Dolls*, the one-of-a-kind figure has a polymer clay head, polymer clay limbs, and a cloth body over a wire armature. Her eyes are porcelain; her face is painted with acrylics. Creating authentic period garb is Batte's specialty: He earned a degree in theater costuming at Baylor University in Texas and taught costume history and design at the College of Santa Fe, and is currently the senior milliner for the San Francisco Opera Company. ൠ

Lady Anne, 23 inches,
polymer clay and cloth, 2000

Elizabethan Bride,
10 inches, hard plastic, 2000

Celebrating bridal fashions throughout history, the Alexander Doll Company's Brides Through the Ages series debuted in 1999 with hard-plastic dolls dressed in gowns inspired by the Rococo, Empire, and Victorian eras. In 2000, the company added two brides representing earlier periods—the Elizabethan and Renaissance eras—to the collection.

In Queen Elizabeth's day, the ladies of the English court were often bedecked in elaborate clothing and jewels. The *Elizabethan Bride* wears a rich gown of lavender brocade. The bodice has long sleeves trimmed at the cuffs with golden mesh. The stomacher (the center front panel) is ivory brocade

flecked with gold thread and is edged with gold and white braid. Around the bride's neck is a ruff—the familiar wheel-shaped collar—of satin ribbon and lace. The gown's skirt has small panniers and a center panel of gold-flecked ivory brocade. The bride's floral lace veil flows from a velvet headpiece covered with gold mesh and edged with gold and white trim. She carries a bouquet of gold and white roses.

The Renaissance was indeed a golden age for costuming. In *Life in the Renaissance* (Random House, 1968) historian Marzieh Gail describes a typical bridal procession of the nobility in a great Italian city:

*Renaissance Bride, 10 inches,
hard plastic, 2000*

Following some archers are trumpeters, pipers and drummers, perhaps two hundred musicians in all. Then come long-robed bishops, ambassadors in black and gold, wearing gold chains and jeweled plumes, followed by a jester, and grooms in purple who lead the bride's dappled gray horse with its gold trappings. Then comes the bride herself on a roan mule, a mule curried, perhaps even rubbed with perfume and wearing a harness covered with roses of fine gold. The bride has yellow hair, gleaming and strung with rubies and pearls, and wears a dress of gold brocade. Four robed men, walking two to each side, hold up a canopy over her head.

The golden-haired *Renaissance Bride* could have stepped right out of this splendid scene. Her gleaming brocade gown has long sleeves of pale-blue crepe trimmed with patterned brocade. The bodice is accented with three rhinestones. She wears an overdress of ivory crushed velvet, tied at the waist with a blue satin bow. Both gown and overdress are edged with golden trim. The bride's cascading veil is English net with ivory Venise lace edging. Her Juliet cap is straw, decorated with sapphire rhinestones and gold braid. Faux sapphire drop earrings and a pearl necklace complete her luxurious look. ✦

The Glove Marriage of Anneke van de Lijn, 18 inches, porcelain and wood, 1996

A wardrobe doll depicting a Dutch bride of 1650, *The Glove Marriage of Anneke van de Lijn*, created by Wendy Lawton for the Lawton Doll Company's Masterpiece Collection, celebrates an age-old custom. "The glove marriage is named for the custom of allowing the bridegroom's exquisitely worked glove to stand proxy at the wedding in his absence," wrote the artist in the Fall/Winter 1996 issue of the Lawton Collectors Guild newsletter. "The glove," she continues, "was sent to the prospective bride's family along with the groom's letter, petition, financial offers and other gifts. Generally, the bride did not know the groom; an intermediary had proposed the match. If the young woman accepted, the wedding would take place while the bride held the glove in the groom's absence."

The fictitious tale of Anneke van de Lijn reflects Lawton's talent for bringing history to life through dolls and storytelling. Just nineteen, Anneke receives a marriage proposal from a wealthy planter—a stranger—who lives in the Dutch East Indies (now Indonesia). Eager for adventure, the spirited young woman says yes. After a marriage ceremony at which her husband is represented by his beaded glove, Anneke embarks on a voyage from her home in the Netherlands to the port city of Batavia (now Jakarta).

Limited to 150, *The Glove Marriage of Anneke van de Lijn* includes the doll (she has a porcelain head and a fully-jointed wood body with porcelain hands); a handpainted wooden trunk; four ensembles; three handcarved dress forms; and a beaded kidskin glove tucked in a mahogany casket. Anneke is shown here wearing her wedding dress, which is gray silk shot with lilac. The bodice has a stomacher of sunset-orange silk trimmed with gilt braid. A lace flounce encircles the neckline; the separate collar (or chemisette) is organdy and lace. Also trimmed in gilt braid, the skirt parts in front to reveal a silk petticoat of the same shade as the stomacher. The bride's wardrobe includes a vermilion linen skirt paired with a deep green basque (a fitted bodice that extends below the waistline), and a cream-colored night clothes set consisting of a batiste chemise, an embroidered cotton sateen basque, and a smocked *robe de chambre*.

Anneke was "a woman of substance," Lawton writes. "How many of her friends would cast aside the expectations of a lifetime to embrace life on a Pacific island halfway around the world?" A woman of substance herself, Lawton made her first doll in 1978. In addition to running her own doll company (with her husband, Keith Lawton), she writes fiction for young readers. ❧

*T*hroughout her distinguished career as a dollmaker, which began in the early 1980s, Israeli artist Edna Dali has made several brides. Most of her ladies are creatures of the imagination, representing no particular era. "In my dolls, I try to transmit feelings: a world of beauty, love, and imagination," she says. For this bride, however, the artist was inspired by the extravagant fashions of late eighteenth-century Europe and America. At that time, the formal gowns of the wealthy were made of luxurious fabrics and had huge hooped skirts and plunging necklines. Hairdos had climbed to hitherto-unknown heights, and could take hours to create.

Made of silk, this bride's gown is embellished throughout with costly antique handmade lace. The beribboned bodice has a low, square-cut neckline finished with lace; the sleeves, also trimmed with lace and ribbon, reach just past the elbows. Two deep flounces of antique lace encircle the gown's full skirt, which is supported by a crinoline. Lace-edged, off-white satin ribbons reach from the waist to the hem, which is trimmed with cream-colored pleated silk ribbon.

Designed and hand-finished by Dali, the bride's enviable ensemble includes a cathedral-length veil fashioned from an antique lace runner and a headpiece of antique wax flowers. Her shoes are leather, and she carries a bouquet of fabric flowers. Her dramatic auburn-colored wig was made by hand out of human hair. "Each hair was individually inserted into the wig cap, which took hours and hours," Dali says. At the forehead, the artist exposed a small piece of the cap, simulating a natural hairline.

The bride's youthful attendants—two bridesmaids and a ring bearer—are dressed in costumes of antique brocade, silk, and taffeta. All four dolls have wax-over-porcelain heads and limbs; their bodies are stuffed cotton over wire, and their eyes are glass.

Made to debut in *Here Come the Bride Dolls*, the one-of-a-kind wedding grouping is titled *The Dream*. Dali muses, "In the bride's eyes one can see a dream come true, but also the unknown...." ∞

*The Dream, 32 inches (bride)
and 11 inches (attendants);
wax-over-porcelain and cloth,
2000*

Johanna, 13½ inches, cloth, 1997

esigned by Oregon-based artist Marilyn Stauber, *Louise*, shown on the opposite page, was inspired by a series of French fashion plates from the early 1830s. "This was a period of extreme femininity," says the artist, who has created more than a dozen dolls depicting bridal fashions. "The 1830s look featured sloping shoulders, leg-of-mutton sleeves, and a full skirt that stopped short of the floor," Stauber says. "Shoes were flat, and hair was worn up off the neck and twisted into braids or high loops with curls on either side of the face."

Made of off-white satin, *Louise*'s gown has a form-fitting bodice embellished at the neckline with lace and fabric flowers and tied at the waist with a long sash that flows down the back. The long sleeves have two large poufs. The full, bell-shaped skirt has three tucks at the bottom and is held out by a lace-trimmed petticoat. (In Stauber's handmade prototype of *Louise*, shown opposite, the skirt was covered by an overlay of lace.) The bride's mohair auburn curls are crowned with a wreath of fabric flowers that secure a lace-edged, floor-length tulle veil. Her ensemble also includes a faux pearl necklace, lace-trimmed pantaloons, and a bouquet of fabric blossoms accented with long satin streamers trimmed with fabric flowers.

Produced in a limited edition of 1,510 by the United States Historical Society of Richmond, Virginia, *Louise* was the souvenir doll for the 48th annual convention of the United Federation of Doll Clubs (UFDC), an international organization for collectors. *Louise* has a porcelain head with a swivel neck, a porcelain upper body, and porcelain arms and legs. (The doll's dainty flat shoes are part of the sculpture.) The bride's body is cloth with a wire armature, and her facial features are painted. Lovely *Louise* was the perfect representation of "To Have and To Hold," the romantically titled theme for the UFDC event.

Preceding the week-long 1997 UFDC conference, which was held in Anaheim, California, was the annual one-day conference of the Original Doll Artists Council of America (ODACA), a group of artists dedicated to improving and promoting their craft. *Johanna*, the souvenir doll for ODACA's "Bridal Tea" luncheon, shown above, was made by Oconto, Wisconsin, artist Kathi Clarke, who loved sewing even as a child. "I was making blazers when other kids were making aprons," she says with a laugh.

Johanna's poseable, floppy body is muslin; her wig is mohair; her eyes and mouth are handpainted. Inspired by late-nineteenth-century bridal styles, Clarke dressed *Johanna* in a gown of ecru lace over ecru taffeta with a high lace collar and leg-of-mutton sleeves. The bride's headpiece is trimmed with fabric roses and dried flowers, which also make up her bouquet. Lace-trimmed pantaloons and a floor-length veil of ecru netting complete *Johanna*'s country-fresh look. The bride is seated comfortably atop a vintage beaded purse (the author's "something borrowed" on her wedding day). ✖

Louise, 15 inches,
porcelain and cloth, 1997
Inset: Louise prototype,
15 inches, porcelain and
cloth, 1995

Right: The Bride Room,
by Henrik Olrik, 1859
Opposite page: The
Bride's Room, 1850s,
13 inches, mixed media,
with detail, 1999

In 1859, Danish artist Henrik Olrik painted a poignant study of a young bride caught in a moment of reflection before her wedding ceremony. Titled *The Bride Room*, the work caught the eye of Maria Åhrén, who specializes in making dolls dressed in historical costumes. A picture of Olrik's painting was included in one of Åhrén's reference books on fashion, and she couldn't resist the challenge of creating a two-doll vignette that captured the contemplative feeling of Olrik's work. "I knew that it would make a beautiful piece," the artist says.

Created in 1999, *The Bride's Room, 1850s* is a fully acces-

sorized scene. The figures, their costumes, and most of the miniature furnishings were handmade by Åhrén. A close study of the painting and the dollmaker's three-dimensional interpretation reveals few differences between the two, particularly in the figures' poses and expressions. "I left out the shawl that's on the table in the painting because I didn't think the color red worked well with the pink that I used for the bridesmaid's dress," the artist says. She also placed a miniature painting over the fireplace instead of the mirror, and gave the bride a bouquet.

Well-versed in historical costuming (Åhrén studied cos-

tume design in Copenhagen and worked in the theater before becoming a full-time dollmaker), the artist carefully recreated the nineteenth-century gowns worn by the bride and her attendant. The bride's gown is white silk with a full skirt. The tightly fitted, pointed bodice has a wide bertha (a shaped collar that falls from a wide oval neckline) trimmed with fringe. The elegant gown is paired with a long tulle veil secured to a wreath of fabric leaves and flowers. The bridesmaid's similarly styled gown is pink silk embellished with white lace. Like the woman in Olrik's painting, she wears a golden necklace.

The Bride's Room, 1850s was limited to an edition of two

(Åhrén always keeps one of each piece for her private collection, which is often displayed in museums). The dolls have sculpted porcelain heads and arms, polyform legs, and fabric bodies with wire armatures. The eyes are handpainted.

Born in Sweden, Åhrén made her first doll at age twelve, out of modeling clay and fabric scraps. "I never stopped making dolls once I started," says the artist, who lives in Minnesota. ಉ

In *Wedding Fashions, 1862-1912: 380 Costume Designs from "La Mode Illustrée"* (Dover Publications, 1994), JoAnne Olian, former curator of the costume collection at the Museum of the City of New York, notes that trappings of the Victorian era were at first "as simple . . . as Victoria's unadorned white satin wedding gown," but then became "increasingly elaborate." A perfect example of mid-nineteenth-century Victorian opulence, *The Victoria and Albert Bride Doll* was introduced in 1989 by The Franklin Mint, a Philadelphia-based direct marketer of history-inspired collectibles. This wedding ensemble with its many embellishments spells luxury from head to toe.

Made of cream-colored taffeta, the gown has a high-necked bodice with a small lace collar and a row of faux pearl buttons. Three ruffles of embroidered lace trim the bodice from the bustline to the waist, which is tied with a taffeta bow that ends in long streamers. The voluminous, two-tiered skirt is decorated with godets (triangular inserts of fabric) covered with embroidered lace. Taffeta bows alternate with the lace-trimmed godets on the bottom tier. The wide sleeves are also embellished with lace-trimmed godets and taffeta bows. In all, more than

forty yards of lace was used in the creation of the gown.

The Victorian bride's ensemble includes an ivory tulle veil with blusher that flows from a wreath of fabric flowers and faux pearls. Underneath the skirt, a lace-trimmed cotton petticoat with two cane hoops gives the gown its full shape. In her hand she carries a posy of satin sweetheart roses.

The Victoria and Albert Bride Doll is porcelain with a cloth torso. Her face is painted; her shoes, part of the porcelain sculpture, are also painted. The bride's hairdo mirrors the fashion of the day: Parted in the center, it's pulled back to show the lower tip of the ears and is gathered into a chignon. A vision of elegance, the doll was inspired by a wedding dress in the collection of The Victoria and Albert Museum in London and was created in cooperation with the museum. ❧

Above: Wedding gowns of 1862 as illustrated by C. Delbomme and Hurot, in the French women's magazine La Mode Illustrée
Opposite page: The Victoria and Albert Bride Doll, 21 inches, porcelain and cloth, 1989

*Opposite page and
above: 1863,
24 inches, polymer clay
and canvas, 1997*

Created by Myra Sherrod, *1863* wears a beautifully decorated bridal gown inspired by Civil War-era fashions. The idea for the gown was born during a visit to a thrift shop, where the artist fell in love with an off-white cotton matelassé (a woven fabric that appears quilted or padded). She had recently sculpted a mature-looking Civil War-era lady, and although she hadn't planned to costume her as a bride, the fabric changed her mind. Referring to historic patterns and fashion books, Sherrod created a dress that she describes as a "compilation of many different features common in that era." The gown is fancier than a typical wartime wedding gown, the artist points out, but adds that "even though the embroidery is elaborate, the design of the dress is simple."

Sherrod decorated the gown with gusto, using antique point d'esprit lace for the flounce on the bodice, the ruffle at the skirt's hem, and the edges of the four tapered panels of the gown's overskirt. Fine silk braid trims the neckline and the cuffs of the sleeves. To add color to the ensemble, the artist embellished the yoke, sleeves, and overskirt panels with silk-ribbon embroidered flowers and leaves in ivory, cream, butter, and light and dark green. The embroidered sections are also beaded with seed pearls.

The one-of-a-kind bride wears a long veil with blusher of point d'esprit lace. It flows from a headpiece of silk leaves and medallions of tiny faux flowers. Green and cream silk ribbon streamers hang from the headpiece and the bouquet, echoing the shades of the embroidered blossoms and leaves. The 1863 bride's costume also includes a full complement of undergarments: a hoop skirt, two petticoats, a chemise, long split drawers, and a lace-up boned corset. In her hands she carries a bouquet of faux field flowers, a lace-trimmed handkerchief (made from a full-size one) and crocheted gloves (shaped by the artist from snippets of vintage doilies).

The doll's head, arms, and legs are sculpted in polymer clay; the body is canvas over a wire armature. Sherrod, who began making dolls in the 1970s, says she "finds pretty dolls boring," and prefers to infuse her sculptures with character. With her upturned head and determined expression, *1863* appears prepared to face the difficulties of her day. "To me, she represents grace under fire," Sherrod says. ❧

A DOUBLE WEDDING
At which Mr. Pipp makes his greatest sacrifice.

An idealized depiction of the fashionable turn-of-the-century American woman, The Gibson Girl was created by Charles Dana Gibson in the 1890s. The artist's work was so influential in his day that "... younger women ... tried to model their clothes, their gestures, their hair and features on the Gibson specifications," wrote Henry C. Pitz, former director of illustration at the Philadelphia College of Art, in his introduction to *The Gibson Girl and Her America* (Dover Publications, 1969).

"The Gibson Girl's clothing was relatively plain with not much in the way of bows and ruffles," says Sheila Wallace McKay, who has spent more than twenty years creating historically accurate costume dolls. Her serene-looking *Gibson Bride* wears a gored gown with a long-trained skirt of cream-colored antique brocade. The gown and the tulle veil, with its faux pearl-studded headpiece, are based on a pair of bridal ensembles shown in an 1899 Gibson illustration. The bride's silhouette is typical of the turn-of-the-century, McKay says. "The emphasis was on an hour-glass shape. The undergarments, which included a bustle and a straight-fronted corset, had to be just right for a dress to fit properly."

The *Gibson Bride*'s undergarments include two petticoats, a corset with "metal" garters (simulated with silver thread), pantaloons, and stockings. A peek under her petticoats also reveals a pair of buckled shoes made of glove leather as well as something blue: a lacy, ribbon-trimmed garter.

McKay began her artistic career as a painter, but found more satisfaction in making dolls depicting fashion ladies and European royalty. Like Madame Tussaud, she uses wax for her three-dimensional portraits. The *Gibson Bride* has a bleached beeswax head and bleached beeswax arms. Her legs are plaster; the body is cloth over wire. Her face is painted with oils and watercolors, and she has implanted-mohair eyebrows and lashes. The bride's pompadour—typical of the Gibson Girl era—is also mohair. ◊

Gibson Bride, detail

Gibson Bride, 15 inches,
wax, cloth, and plaster,
1992

From Garçonne to Glamour

⦿⦿⦿⦿⦿⦿⦿⦿⦿⦿⦿⦿⦿⦿⦿⦿⦿⦿⦿⦿⦿⦿⦿⦿⦿⦿⦿⦿⦿

omen's fashions changed drastically in the 1920s. By the middle of the decade, skirt hems had climbed to just below the knee. Women bobbed their hair, danced the Charleston, and celebrated their increased personal and political freedom. The boyish, curve-concealing couture of the 1920s, sometimes called the *garçonne*, is beautifully expressed in *Caroline*, a Roaring Twenties bride. Created by Stephanie Blythe, she was inspired by the artist's grandmother, an actress who met her husband in Paris. "She died when my mother was still young girl, and there are very few photos of her," Blythe says. "The ones that exist show a woman who is dainty and winsome with that wondrous charm that seems to hold captive the secret of enduring youth."

Using vintage issues of *Vogue* as a reference guide, Blythe created an ensemble that her grandmother might have worn on her wedding day. "I wanted it to be well-designed and beautifully cut with a single idea in its construction, and only such trimmings as to give it character," the artist says. In her design she incorporated the key elements that distinguish the Parisian-made bridal frocks of the 1920s: the straight, tubular shape that deemphasized the bust and hips; the elongated waistline; and an overall feeling of richness without clutter.

Caroline's dress is made of silk with an overlayer of patterned lace netting embellished with tiny pearls. The dress ends below the knee in a tiered decorative hem. A long strand of pearls gives shimmer to the neckline. The bride wears textured silk stockings; her silk shoes are trimmed with bows and golden buckles. Typical of the period, *Caroline*'s pearl-edged veil is long, banded low on the forehead with a narrow band of pearl-trimmed lace, and secured on either side of the head with a finely embroidered vintage lace leaf.

A graduate of the Philadelphia College of Art, Blythe worked in textile and graphic design before sculpting her first doll in the early 1980s. For more than a decade her dolls were made in partnership with artist Susan Snodgrass; in 1996, Blythe began creating dolls on her own. Well-known for her artful porcelain renderings of ladies, lovers, fairies, and sprites, Blythe created *Caroline* especially for debut in *Here Come the Bride Dolls*. The one-of-a-kind doll has a sculpted porcelain head, sculpted porcelain arms and legs, and a wired, cloth body. Her wig is mohair, and her eyes are handpainted by the artist. ❧

*Caroline, 10½ inches,
porcelain and cloth, 2000*

Three brides from the Alexander Doll Company illustrate the different styles of wedding attire donned during the 1920s. From 1999, the *Roaring 20s Bride*, shown on the opposite page, top left, wears the most familiar fashion: the short and sassy flapper-style dress. Hers is ivory charmeuse. The bodice is trimmed with Cluny lace and embellished with an embroidered appliqué panel studded with rhinestones. Pink ribbon roses add color at the neckline and hip. A long train—popular throughout the 1920s—is trimmed with ribbon roses, lace, and pink ribbon. Made of hard plastic, the doll wears a train-length veil of pale-pink English net secured with ribbon roses.

First calf-length, then knee-length, skirts returned to the floor by the end of the decade. But in between there was a transition period, when uneven hemlines were the rage. The peach gown worn by the bride above has such a hemline; hers is raised in front with a point, and long in back. Inspired by a real Parisian-made dress from 1928 (a ceremonial dress worn for presentation before King George V at the Court of Saint James's), the gown is embellished with ribbon flowers in various hues. Fashioned of pale-peach satin covered with lace, the gorgeous gown is paired

with an equally stunning veil. Made of lace embroidered with a floral pattern of peach and green, the veil is further accented with ribbon flowers.

A one-of-a-kind doll, the untitled bride was made in 1993 for auction at the annual Walt Disney World Doll and Teddy Bear Convention. She has a vinyl head and arms, and a hard-plastic body and legs. The bride is accompanied by two attendants: a ring bearer in a brocade sailor suit and a flower girl in satin and lace. Both attendants are hard plastic.

Introduced in 1995, the *1920s Bride*, shown on the opposite page, top right, celebrates the return of femininity to fashion by the end of the decade. Her flowing gown of lace over taffeta is tied at the waist with a satin sash adorned with a satin bloom. The demure-looking, hard-plastic bride wears a long veil of point d'esprit lace.

As shown by these dolls and by bride Vincenza DiLeonardi, who wed Luigi Ferraro in New York City on December 12, 1920, the Twenties bride usually wore a very long veil, whether her dress was long or short. Also popular were huge bouquets trimmed with flower-sprinkled ribbon streamers. ☙

Opposite page: Untitled bride with attendants, 21 inches and 8 inches, vinyl and hard plastic (bride), hard plastic (attendants), 1993
Below left: Roaring 20s Bride, 10 inches, hard plastic, 1999
Below: 1920s Bride, 10 inches, hard plastic, 1995
Bottom: Wedding party of 1920

The brainchild of Mel Odom, an award-winning illustrator with *Time* and *OMNI* covers to his credit, Gene is a ficti-tious movie star who graced the silver screen from the 1940s through the early 1960s. Gene dons a circa-1926 wedding ensemble for *The Legend of Ida Best*, in which she portrays a silent-screen star who weds a count. "With this costume, I tried to capture the spirit of the 1920s," says Tim Kennedy, the New York City clothing designer who created *I Do*, shown on the opposite page. It's the 1920s, but with a twist: "Because *I Do* is supposed to be a movie costume, it's really a 1940s *interpretation* of a 1920s dress. The waistline, for example, is more fitted than it would have been in the twenties," Kennedy explains.

Graceful and fluid, *I Do* has a lightly gathered bodice with a dipped asymmetrical neckline. Looped ribbons lead from a cluster of ribbon rosettes at the neckline to another cluster at the hip. Layered lace panniers adorn the skirt. Gene's cascading lace veil flows from a lace cap trimmed with ribbon rosettes. The ensemble also includes short gloves, strappy shoes, and a bouquet of faux lilies.

Gene is produced by the Ashton-Drake Galleries of Niles, Illinois, a direct marketer of dolls. She is made of vinyl and has painted blue eyes. A collector of fashion dolls and a film aficionado, Odom developed Gene to fulfill his own wish for a doll dressed in well-crafted miniature versions of mid-twentieth-century haute couture. Boasting a to-die-for wardrobe of fully-accessorized ensembles, Gene made her unforgettable grand entrance into the world of fashion dolls in 1995.

Odom has a passion for 1920s fashions, so it's no sur-prise that *I Do* is one of his favorite Genes. He laments that the beautifully crafted clothing of the 1920's was rendered obsolete by the outbreak of the Depression in 1929. "They were like party clothes for a party that stopped abruptly and never happened again," he says wistfully.

I Do debuted in 2000 in an edition of 5,000. Introduced that same year were the *Will You Marry Me?* costume (designed by José Ferrand)—which Gene wears for the big proposal scene in *The Legend of Ida Best*—and the *Bon Voyage* doll, who wears a dashing honeymoon travel ensemble (designed by George Sarofeen). ∞

Above: Will You Marry Me?,
15½ inches, vinyl, 2000
Above left: Bon Voyage, 15½ inches,
vinyl, 2000
Opposite: I Do, 15½ inches, vinyl, 2000

Influenced by Hollywood glamour and the angular lines of Art Deco, 1930s bridal wear was often sensual and dramatic. Bias-cut, body-hugging gowns were popular, as demonstrated by the doll *Kathleen* and by real-life bride Sophie DiFabio, who wed Thomas Martin Gorman in 1931. The bodice of *Kathleen*'s satin gown has a rolled neckline with an embroidered lace insert. Triple strands of crystal beads drape down the sleeves, which end in points. The skirt has a tight, gathered hipline. Below the knee, the skirt flares into a fishtail shape. *Kathleen* has Hollywood-style makeup, with narrow, finely arched eyebrows and ruby-red lips. Her tulle veil flows from a Juliet cap of faux pearls and beads, and she carries a posy of fabric roses.

 Kathleen was the third issue in the Classic Brides of the Century collection produced by Ashton-Drake Galleries in partnership with Roman, Inc., a Chicago-based giftware company. The dolls were based on figurines created by the late Ellen Williams, a giftware designer with a flair for fashion. *Kathleen* has a porcelain head and shoulder plate, porcelain arms and legs, and a cloth body. She was introduced and retired in 1993. ℕ

Left: Kathleen, 18 inches, porcelain and cloth, 1993
Below: The June 14, 1931, wedding party of Sophie DiFabio and Thomas Martin Gorman

Victoria, 21 inches, resin and cloth, 1994

The modest gown worn by *Victoria* was inspired by the understated elegance of late 1940s bridal wear. Popular with many brides of that decade were heart-shaped "sweetheart" necklines, wide and padded shoulders, and full skirts. Made of cotton moiré, *Victoria*'s trained gown is trimmed at the neckline and dropped waistline with a band of lace and faux pearls, and at the back with a pearl-trimmed bow. The long sleeves end in points. Two lace ruffles accent the bottom center of the skirt; a third trims the hem. The train-length tulle veil flows from a tiara of lace and faux pearls. Tulle and ribbons decorate the bride's bouquet of fabric blooms.

Part of the Daddy's Long Legs line, *Victoria* was produced by KVK Inc., the Southlake, Texas, company founded by Karen and Brent Germany. Marilyn Wade sculpted the prototype; Karen Germany designed the costume. *Victoria* has a resin head, resin torso, and resin lower arms and legs; her upper limbs are cloth. Her hair is sculpted and her eyes are painted. Introduced in 1994, the bride was later joined by a groom, *Maurice*, and two attendants, *Maggie*, the flower girl, and *Joshua*, the ring bearer. *Victoria* was limited to an edition of 2500, which closed in 1995. ଧ

Two of the most famous twentieth-century brides—Grace Kelly and Jacqueline Bouvier—wed in the 1950s, a decade of postwar prosperity and bridal luxury. Young women donned romantic, feminine gowns. Billowy skirts, padded busts, and cinched waistlines were popular, as were pastel colors.

In the fictitious film *Monaco*, Mel Odom's Gene plays a young American who marries a European prince (à la Grace Kelly). Timothy Alberts, a costume supervisor in the motion picture industry, designed Gene's quintessential 1950s wedding dress. The short-sleeved lace-over-satin bodice ("it's very demure," says Alberts) and full tulle skirt are classic elements of 1950s-era bridal attire, he notes. But it was nineteenth-century Russian court costume—specifically, a halo-style headdress called a "*kokoshnik*"—that inspired Gene's pearl-trimmed headpiece. The *Monaco* ensemble also includes a long tulle veil, a net slip, seamed white hose, white strappy heels, faux pearl jewelry, and a bouquet of white fabric blossoms.

"I think that many mothers and grandmothers of Gene collectors wore wedding gowns resembling *Monaco*," Alberts says. He's right: minus the ribbon roses sprinkled on the skirt (in Alberts' prototype, shown here for the first time in print, the flowers were larger), Gene's dress is nearly a mirror image of the gown worn by the author's mother, Bernice Fecher, née Pottok, for her April 18, 1953, marriage to Walter Fecher. The history of Mrs. Fecher's gown is a New York story rather than a Hollywood fairy tale: her dress was purchased in Martin's, a now-defunct Brooklyn department store.

Made of vinyl, *Monaco* was introduced in 1995 and retired two years later. According to A. Glenn Mandeville, a leading authority on fashion dolls, a mint example of this Gene bride brought about $195 on the secondary market in 2000, more than double her original retail price of $69.95. ◊

Above left: Timothy Alberts' original design for Monaco
Above: Bernice Fecher on her April 18, 1953, wedding day
Opposite page: Monaco, 15½ inches, vinyl, 1995

With her dashing, pillbox hat headpiece, Beth is easily recognizable as a bride of the 1960s. Introduced in 1995 by the Ashton-Drake Galleries, *Beth's 1960s Wedding Dress* is part of the From This Day Forward collection, which tells the sentimental, make-believe story of an heirloom bridal gown worn and cherished by four generations of American women.

The story begins with Elizabeth, who weds in 1900. Her gown has a high-necked bodice with a lace bertha-style collar, leg-of-mutton sleeves capped with lace, and a long-trained, bell-shaped skirt. Her daughter, Betty, makes her walk down the aisle in the 1930s. To make her mother's gown more stylish, she has the train and skirt drawn in to create an elongated silhouette. The tulle veil of 1900 flowed from a flowered headpiece; the 1930s version is partially gathered atop a sleek satin cap.

Beth, the 1960s bride, dramatically changes the gown's neckline, preferring an off-the-shoulder, wrapped portrait style. She opts for a flyaway net veil instead of a long tulle one, and accents her ensemble with wrist-length gloves (a popular accessory for the Sixties bride). Lisa, the 1990s bride, brings the story full circle. She replaces the portrait neckline with a high collar and lace flounce. The leg-of-mutton sleeves are back, as is the chapel-length train. The skirt's scalloped hem, trimmed with peach blossoms and bows in 1900, is now accented with dainty pink bows dotted with faux pearls. Like many modern brides, Lisa clearly favors the flavor of the past.

The From this Day Forward dolls were designed by Phil Tumminio, who ran a family-based doll manufacturing business. Each bride has a porcelain head, porcelain chest plate, porcelain limbs, and a cloth torso. ❧

Opposite page: Beth's 1960s Wedding Dress, 16 inches seated, 1995
Above from left: Betty's 1930s Wedding Dress, 19 inches, 1995; Beth's 1960s Wedding Dress; Elizabeth's 1900s Wedding Dress, 19 inches, 1995
Right: Lisa's 1990s Wedding Dress, 19 inches, 1995
All dolls are porcelain and cloth.

The "swinging singles" culture emerged in the late 1960s, when many young men and women rebelled against the mainstream. *Beth*, a hippie bride, has eschewed tradition in favor of a flower child look. Created by British artist Gillie Charlson, she wears a romantic dress of patterned chiffon accented with burgundy chiffon at the hem, neckline, and upper sleeves. The bride's mohair tresses are crimped, with two braids interwoven with strips of the patterned chiffon. Her bouquet, made of flowers that she picked herself, is tied with chiffon. Like many free-spirited 1960s brides, *Beth* celebrated her wedding outdoors. "I can just imagine her dancing barefoot as her dress swirls around her," says Charlson. Introduced in an edition of ten, *Beth* has a poured wax head, upper body, and limbs; her body is cloth and wire.

The 1970s bride shown on the opposite page is a collaboration between dollmaker Robert Tonner and retired fashion designer Frank Rizzo. A graduate of New York City's Parson's School of Design, Rizzo became an instructor at the school in 1966 (his students included Tonner and Donna Karan); he also served as Chair of Fashion Design for over a decade. As a designer, Rizzo specialized in bridal wear. In the 1970s, he traveled around the United States, unveiling his innovative, award-winning designs in upscale department stores and bridal salons. He recalls: "We had just come out of the sixties, with all this hippie, anti-formal wedding, let's-get-married-in-the-park thing. And here was a resurgence of young girls, maybe eighteen or nineteen, who had done the park thing and now wanted to get married in proper, pretty clothes—this time in a church."

In 1995, Tonner invited fashion designers to create one-of-a-kind costumes for his vinyl American Models. (These designer dolls were auctioned to benefit various charities.) For his model, Rizzo recreated one of his most popular 1970s bride gowns: a shimmering ice-blue confection. Rizzo painstakingly stitched hundreds of tiny sequins and crystals to the silk bodice. Beads and sequins also adorn the tulle overskirt (the underskirt is silk duchesse satin). A beaded tiara and a floor-length tulle veil complete the sophisticated look.

When Rizzo designed this gown in the 1970s, his aim was to introduce bridal couture to a generation of young women who'd never worn a dress. The gown worked magic. Rizzo recalls the look on many a young woman's face as she tried it on: "They were transformed," he says, "into fairy princesses." ✍

Beth, 23 inches, wax and cloth, 2000

In the 1980s, hairdos were big, and so were weddings. The fairytale wedding of Lady Diana Spencer and Princes Charles on July 29, 1981, set the tone for the decade. Bridal glamour was back, with a vengeance. Created by the Ashton-Drake Galleries in partnership with Roman, Inc., *Jennifer, The 1980s Bride* was the third issue in the Classic Brides of the Century collection by Ellen Williams. Her satin, sheath-style gown has an attached train, a sweetheart neckline, and leg-of-mutton sleeves, and is lavishly trimmed with lace, iridescent beads, and faux pearls. Asymmetrical in shape, the elaborate headpiece is adorned with fabric flowers and cascading sprays of faux pearls. The floor-length tulle veil is gathered above the head into a fan-shaped pouf.

"In my mind, Jennifer was seeking real glamour in her bridal wear. As a young woman of the 1980s, she felt confident enough to let her own personality express itself," the late Williams said. Introduced in 1991 and retired the following year, *Jennifer* has a porcelain head, upper body, lower arms and legs, and a cloth body. Her eyes are painted. ✤

Jennifer, The 1980s Bride, 19½ inches, porcelain and cloth, 1991

A tribute to 1980s opulence, *Kristina* is an all-porcelain doll by Marilyn Stauber. The bride's gown is made of cream silk and satin. The waist is tied with a sash, and a row of neat pearl buttons that really open and close extends from wrist to elbow on each tight-fitting sleeve. (The gown has a row of working buttons down the back as well.) The bustline and shoulders are covered by a sumptuous lace cape embellished by the artist with pearls, crystals, sequins, and blue beads. Finished with a scalloped edge, the cape is edged with a beaded fringe. The cape falls to the ground, forming a train that extends beyond the gown's train. Completing *Kristina*'s ensemble are a silk veil held in place by a crown of flowers and an oversized bouquet.

Kristina was limited to ten, but each doll in the edition was costumed, wigged, and painted differently. The doll is jointed at the neck, hips, knees and waist, and her features are handpainted by the artist. ❧

Kristina, 27 inches, porcelain, 1987

Modern Love

"The names of the fabrics intoxicate: silk faille, gazar, cloque, moiré, chiffon, shantung; the laces enchant: Alençon, Chantilly, Honiton," writes Maria McBride-Mellinger, former fashion editor of *Bride's*, in *The Perfect Wedding* (Collins SanFrancisco, 1997). The modern bride can wear a gown of any material, in any style she chooses. Snow white or blush pink, formal or informal, revealing or conservative, contemporary bride gowns, like the women who don them, are free of restrictions.

One of the most successful makers of contemporary bride dolls is the Robert Tonner Doll Company based in Hurley, New York. Its founder, Robert Tonner, brings a keen sense of style to his creations. The Indiana-born artist earned a BFA degree at Parson's School of Design in New York City and honed his skills as a sportswear designer for Bill Blass. But Tonner had another dream: a doll enthusiast, he wanted to create his own miniature fashion mannequins. He began sculpting in 1980; eleven years later, he left Seventh Avenue to make dolls full-time. In 1992, Tonner's company was born.

In 1999, Tonner introduced Tyler Wentworth, a fashion doll made of vinyl and hard plastic. The director of the House of Wentworth, Tyler designs—and wears—a chic, New York City-style wardrobe. For *Here Come the Bride Dolls*, Tonner created two spectacular dolls: his first-ever Tyler Wentworth brides.

"This is how I love to see a bride: gorgeous, gorgeous, fabric, and not a lot of fussy detail," Tonner says of the one-of-a-kind Tyler, shown on the opposite page. She wears a gown of ivory silk shantung with reversed sequin embroidery. The wrapped bodice has a décolleté neckline; at the waist is a shirred cummerbund. A floor-length tulle veil, faux pearl choker, and a bouquet of ceramic lilies and roses complete the ensemble. The first Tyler with bendable arms, she also has one-of-a-kind face paint by noted doll painter Sherry Miller.

Fashion Show Finale, shown at right, was introduced in 2001 in an edition of 500 and wears a tiered, trained gown of embroidered tulle. The fitted bodice is lightly beaded and has organza ribbon straps tied with bows. "I see this gown being worn at a daytime summer wedding—a garden wedding," Tonner muses. This Tyler ensemble includes beaded shoes, a floor-length tulle veil, a bouquet, and a pair of long gloves—the perfect accent for a sleeveless gown. 🎀

Fashion Show Finale, 16 inches, vinyl and hard plastic, 2001

Sharon Stone, Holly Hunter, and Uma Thurman: three very different women, with three unique looks. Yet when each of these lovely luminaries took her vows, she did so wearing a Vera Wang. Since 1990, when Wang's salon opened its doors at the Carlyle Hotel in Manhattan, her name has become synonymous with contemporary bridal chic. A chic lady herself, Barbie donned a Vera Wang in 1998. Made exclusively for Barbie by the New York City-based designer to the stars, the gown is a dream rendered in silk duchesse satin.

"I wanted the final effect to be glamorous and epic," Wang says. The biggest challenge in designing for Barbie, she admits, was determining the appropriate style for the gown. "This gown needed to be timeless and appeal to all of Barbie's fans—the entire spectrum of her collectors, from little girls to adults." After several discussions with Barbie, Wang created a gown that incorporates many of the traditional elements for which she is known—a ball gown skirt, exquisite detail, and luxurious fabrics—yet "still exudes a modern sensibility."

Artful and precise in its lines, the gown has a halter-style bodice framed with a narrow band of black velvet piping. ("The black velvet trim is not typically used with wedding gowns," Wang notes.) The back, shoulders, and sleeves are sheer illusion. Also edged with black piping, the skirt opens in back, revealing a trained insert panel. Barbie wears a triple-layer tulle veil with blusher, which billows from a dainty velvet bow. Completing the ensemble are a tulle petticoat, faux pearl earrings, stockings, garter, and a posy of red roses.

During her twenty-five-plus years in the fashion industry (before launching her label, Wang served as senior fashion editor at *Vogue* and design director for Ralph Lauren), Vera Wang has met and mingled with glamorous, self-assured women from all walks of life. Of all these formidable females, Barbie was one of the most memorable. "Compared to the other celebrities that I have had the honor to work with, Barbie was the ideal client," Wang says. "Barbie loved the style of gown that I designed, and her fittings went flawlessly well!"

The *Vera Wang Barbie* introduced a series of glamorous dolls designed by Vera Wang. Included with the doll was a reproduction of the designer's original sketch for the gown. &

Vera Wang Barbie,
11½ inches, vinyl,
1998

*I*n 1997 the Alexander Doll Company debuted a collection of Cissy dolls dressed in vibrant floral fashions. Cissy in her *Peony & Butterfly Wedding Gown* is a testament to the anything-goes attitude of the modern bride. Made of pink-and-white silk dupioni gingham trimmed with handbeaded lace, the short dress with its gauzy pale-pink yoke is framed by a tiered train. Fabric peonies and feather butterflies crown her headpiece; some friendly butterflies have also alighted on her train.

Perfect for a springtime wedding, the ensemble includes elbow-length gloves, a pink tulle flyaway veil, a bouquet of daises, and butterfly jewelry. Cissy, Madame Alexander's classic haute couture creation, debuted in 1952; the *Peony & Butterfly Wedding Gown* Cissy is vinyl with bendable hard-plastic legs and sleep eyes. ᴈᴑ

Peony & Butterfly Wedding Gown,
21 inches, vinyl and hard plastic, 1997

Now and Forever,
15½ inches, vinyl, 2000

Well-known for creating dolls that depict lovable babies and children for her Connecticut-based company, Susan Wakeen debuted Eve, a glamorous fashion figure, in 2000. A famous photo journalist, Eve boasts a wardrobe of contemporary clothing. Stylish, sensual, and sleek, the *Now and Forever* Eve wears a wedding ensemble that's sure to turn heads. "I wanted to represent sweetness yet maturity," the artist says. The bustier-style bodice of silk shantung has narrow shoulder straps and a dropped waistline; the full, swirling skirt is satin.

To emphasize the gown's lean lines, Wakeen kept the decoration simple: a satin bow and a row of silk and organza rosebuds adorn the bodice; fabric flowers also trim the edge of Eve's gloves. The ensemble includes faux pearl jewelry, a nosegay of white roses, and a chapel-length tulle veil with blusher that cascades from a cluster of organza blooms. The *Now and Forever* bride is vinyl with painted eyes, and was introduced by Susan Wakeen, Inc., in an edition of 2,500. ❧

Here Comes the Bride, front and side views, 17 inches, polyform clay and fabric, 1998

Serene and lovely, Antonette Cely's modern bride is posed as if listening to the opening strains of the wedding march. Titled *Here Comes the Bride*, she was commissioned by health and fitness advocate Richard Simmons, an avid doll collector, in 1998. "I wanted something very traditional," Simmons says. "I wanted pearls around her neck; I wanted her to hold a bouquet; I wanted a veil over her face."

For the doll's gown, Cely found inspiration in *Sabrina*, one of her favorite romantic films. In a scene in which Sabrina turns heads and wins hearts, the lithe Audrey Hepburn wears a stunning sheath dress with an overskirt. The artist adapted this style to the bride's gown, fashioning both sheath and overskirt out of raw silk. Using an exquisite piece of antique lace from Switzerland, the artist added a second overskirt that forms a long train. She created the bride's veil out of tulle; the headband is modeled in clay and covered with silk.

Cely's professional experience as a costume designer and makeup artist for film and theater has served her well in her career as a dollmaker, which began in 1982. Like miniature actors, her figures appear graceful and poised, with their expressions and poses telling the viewer a story. *Here Comes the Bride*, a one-of-a-kind work, is a blend of several media. The head is polyform clay covered with broadcloth; the torso, arms, and legs are broadcloth over a carefully shaped understructure of batting and wire. The artist made the bride's hairdo out of mohair, which she hand-dyed; the eyes are handpainted. ✤

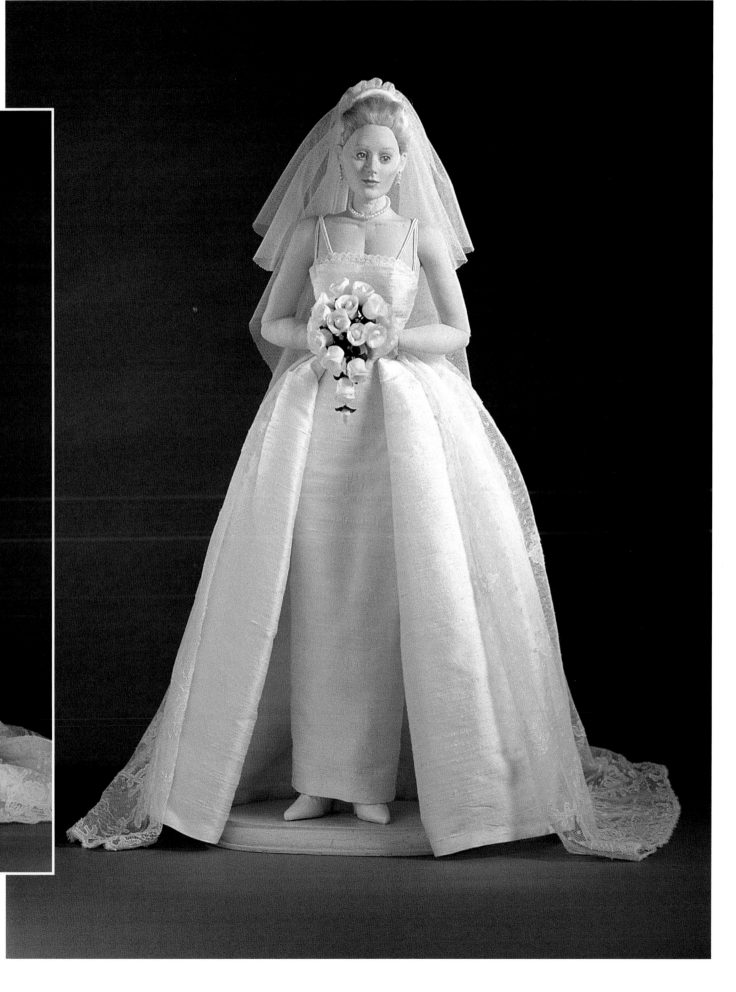

Two charming brides—one traditional, the other up-to-the-minute—illustrate the disparate styles of contemporary bridal wear. Both dolls were made by Corolle, the French firm whose name means "the heart of a flower." *Angelique, "La Mariée,"* ("the bride" in French), shown on the opposite page, produced in 1992, wears the formal, long-sleeved style favored by many brides. Made of taffeta, the gown has a high-necked lace collar with a lace bertha. The sleeves are lace with large taffeta poufs. The skirt has a lace apron with a ruffled, embroidered lace hem dotted with faux pearls. A wreath of fabric flowers and a train-length tulle veil edged with intricately patterned lace complete the bride's romantic look. *Angelique* was designed by Catherine Refabert, who, together with husband Jacques Refabert, founded Corolle in 1979.

Refabert retired in 1996 and was succeeded by Catherine Petot, a former children's fashion designer. In 1999, Petot created *La Mariée*, a limited edition of 750, shown at right. Simple, smart, and semiformal, her satin dress has a square neckline and capped sleeves. A satin rosette accents the waistline. The gown is complemented by a chic wrap of embroidered lace, a simple headpiece of fabric flowers, and a faux pearl necklace.

The Corolle brides are vinyl and have glass eyes, human-hair wigs, and human-hair eyelashes. Like all of the company's dolls, they are produced in the Loire Valley, a storybook setting of magnificent castles and gardens. Both of these sweet-faced brides reflect Catherine Refabert's founding philosophy for the firm: to make dolls "for the collector's eye and the child's heart." ❧

Right: La Mariée, 22 inches, vinyl, 1999
Opposite page: Angelique,
"La Mariée," 21 inches, vinyl, 1992

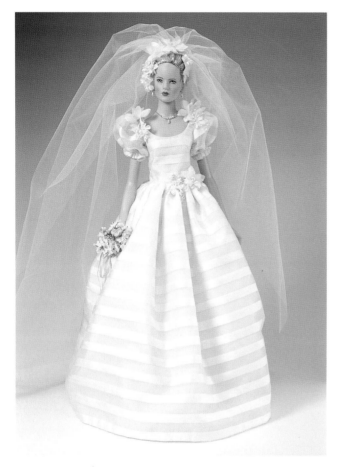

*G*illian, Robert Tonner's first bride, shown above left, was inspired, like many of his dolls, by a gorgeous fabric—in this case, a satin-stripe silk organza. Tonner describes *Gillian*'s gown as "classic contemporary," which he defines as a modern design with a nostalgic feeling. Other than a sprinkling of silk flowers at the waist and shoulders, the gown has little adornment; the shimmering fabric and the sleek, simple design do all the talking. Tasteful faux pearl jewelry and a billowy floor-length tulle veil attached to an asymmetrical headpiece of silk flowers complete *Gillian*'s timeless, romantic look.

In 1996, one year after *Gillian*'s debut, Tonner introduced *Beverly*, shown above right. He chose the gown's main fabric—an embroidered organza—because the criss-cross pattern in the material made him think of a garden trellis, a popular accent for outdoor weddings. The bodice has a scalloped neckline and a cummerbund of tissue-taffeta. The petal-shaped skirt parts in front, revealing a slim taffeta underskirt. *Beverly* is framed by a veil of tulle attached to a headpiece trimmed with faux pearls.

Colette, shown on the opposite page, introduced in 1997,

was a breakthrough piece for the artist/designer. "She set the tone for the line," Tonner explains. "She was much more embellished than anything I'd ever done. After *Colette*, everything got more elaborate: costuming, hair, makeup."

Colette's gown is organza over cream-colored satin. Fit for a princess, the organza is richly embroidered with seed pearls and sequins. Slightly A line in shape, the trained gown has long sleeves ending in points over the hands and a scalloped hem. A chic hooded floor-length cape of cream satin and a draped tulle scarf complete the ensemble. *Colette* was offered in both white and African-American versions.

Gillian was issued in an edition of 500; *Beverly* and *Colette* were each limited to 750 pieces. All three vinyl brides have painted eyes and were part of Tonner's innovative, fashion-forward American Model Collection. ✍

Above left: Gillian, 20 inches, vinyl, 1995
Above: Beverly, 20 inches, vinyl, 1996
Opposite page: Colette, 20 inches, vinyl, 1997

*M*illennium Bride Barbie symbolizes two magical beginnings: the dawn of a new century, and a celebration of marriage. Beautiful and bejeweled, Barbie wears a bridal ensemble created by dynamic Mattel designer Robert Best. A graduate of New York City's Parson's School of Design, Best worked as a designer for Isaac Mizrahi for four years before joining Mattel in 1995. For the *Millennium Bride*, Best artfully combined silver satin and tulle, then showered the dream dress with beads, sequins, and Swarovski crystals. The gown's cape-like back cascades from the shoulders into a sweeping train; the veil, dotted with rhinestones, flows from a tiara. Introduced in 2000 in a numbered edition of 10,000, *Millennium Bride Barbie* carries a shimmering bouquet of silver roses. ∽

Millennium Bride Barbie,
11½ inches, vinyl, 2000

With her garden-fresh fabrics and fashions, Laura Ashley brought the charm of the English countryside to homes all around the world. In 1995, Mattel celebrated the work of the Welsh-born designer with a collection of dolls garbed in Laura Ashley-inspired ensembles. *Rosalind*, the bride, was a vision of elegance in her traditional and tasteful ivory satin and lace gown. Falling gracefully from a floral headpiece, the fingertip-length tulle veil is edged in satin ribbon. *Rosalind*'s clas-

sic ensemble also includes satin slippers, a faux pearl necklace, a blue garter, and a bouquet. The doll has a vinyl head, vinyl limbs, a vinyl upper body, and a fabric torso and was packaged with a story booklet. ☙

Rosalind, 26 inches, vinyl and cloth, 1995

Left: June Bride, 28 inches, poured wax, 1998

Above and opposite page: Cappucine, 28 inches, poured wax, 1998

Captivating *Cappucine*, shown above right and on the opposite page, is one of the many glamorous brides created by British dollmaking duo Paul Crees and Peter Coe. "Every bride looks beautiful on her wedding day, and this is a wonderful thing to capture in essence," says Crees.

Caught in a reverie, *Cappucine* is as dreamy as her exquisite gown, which is made out of cream silk accented with a golden trellis pattern. The sleeveless bodice is covered with a cream-silk bolero decorated with lace, faux pearls, and iridescent sequins. Adding further drama to the ensemble are a wide-brimmed hat made of the same patterned silk as the dress and edged all around with lace; a draping of silk tulle covers the hat and forms a train.

Cappucine was introduced in 1998 in an edition of ten along with the equally lovely *June Bride*, an edition of five. *June*

Bride wears a gown of peach silk brocade with a floral pattern. The sleeveless bodice and matching bolero are decorated with clusters of iridescent sequins and faux pearls. Her wide-brimmed hat, made of the dress fabric, is similarly embellished. *June Bride* wears a silk tulle veil and carries a bouquet of peach silk blooms.

With more than twenty years of dollmaking behind them, Crees and Coe are well-known for their stunning feminine figures, which are made of wax and handpainted. As youngsters, both artists were entranced by the theater. The pair met when they both landed jobs at the Theatre Royal in Bristol, England's oldest working theater. Their shared love of plays and films is evident in their creations, which often appear caught in the middle of a dramatic performance. ✌

Dorothy Hoskins celebrates two moods of modern matrimony with these miniature works. *Last Minute*, shown on the opposite page, is a humorous homage to the delightful chaos of the Big Day. Not yet happily married, the happily *harried* bride is frantically putting on her shoes. Someone is knocking on her bedroom door, reminding her that it's time to go! Hoskins came up with the idea for this doll after receiving a damaged 1920s wedding gown from one of her daughters, who spotted the tattered frock in London. "The lace was so beautiful that I wanted to use it in a way that would show as much of the pattern as possible," Hoskins says. Creating a wedding gown, she decided, was the perfect way to show off the vintage lace in all its glory. As skilled at making miniature garments as she is at sculpting diminutive dolls—*Last Minute* is just 4¾ inches tall—Hoskins turned the silk satin petticoat of the real gown into the underlayer of the doll's dress. She covered the satin with lace salvaged from the full-sized gown; the same lace adorns the doll's wee slippers. For a final touch, the artist created a billowy veil out of the 1920s gown's chiffon lining.

Wedding Bloom, shown above, depicts another bride's private moment. This bride takes things slowly, turning her final preparations into a sensuous dance of joy. Lovingly she raises her gossamer veil over her head, letting its folds drape around her, as if the veil itself is a partner in the dance. Like real-life bride Grace Gavigan, who wed James Azzara on October 30, 1993, she is lost in a reverie.

Made especially for debut in *Here Come the Bride Dolls*, *Wedding Bloom* is a one-of-a-kind version of one of the artist's limited-edition resin dolls. For the costume, Hoskins parted with a long-cherished piece of heirloom Battenburg lace. Combining the lace with silk satin left over from the 1920s wedding gown, she concocted a trained, sleeveless gown with a slender silhouette. The shoulder straps are triple bands of vintage seed pearls; the veil is silk edged with tatted lace ("the smallest I've ever seen," the artist notes).

Hoskins, who resides in Alaska, made her first doll in the early 1980s. She creates a variety of dolls but is best-known for her miniatures, which are pure magic. ✺

*Opposite page: Wedding Bloom,
5½ inches, resin, 2000
Above: Last Minute, 4¾ inches,
porcelain, 1999
Right: Grace Azzara née Gavigan on
her October 30, 1993, wedding day*

*To Have and To Hold, 21 inches,
vinyl and hard plastic, 2000*

Created for debut in *Here Come the Bride Dolls*, this exquisite one-of-a-kind Cissy bride, called *To Have and To Hold*, walks down the aisle courtesy of the Alexander Doll Company. "The inspiration for this doll actually came from the material," says Linda Sankovich, the designer of the luxurious gown. "I was lucky enough to be able to purchase some re-embroidered laces from sample cards used by a bridal company. The lace wasn't beaded, but each had a beautiful pattern. When I layered some pink chiffon over white satin, then placed the lace over both fabrics, I was inspired to make this gown." To make the dress even more sumptuous, Sankovich painstakingly hand-beaded each piece of the lace with pearls and sequins. "There are approximately one hundred hours of beading in the dress," she says. "The skirt alone took several months to complete."

Made of pink silk satin covered with beaded lace, the bodice is sleeveless with a halter-style neckline and a dropped waist. The back is trimmed with a cluster of handmade fabric roses and beaded lace. The full skirt with its cathedral-length train is pink chiffon over white satin, elaborately trimmed with beaded lace. There's an underskirt of pink silk satin and a petticoat made from stiff white netting and trim lace.

The bride's upswept platinum-blonde hairdo leads the eye to a crown of Swarovksi crystal rhinestones and pearls. The fingertip-length veil and blusher are tulle edged in white cord. Cissy's ensemble includes shoes, gloves, drop earrings, and a ribbon-tied bouquet made of pastel-colored bread-dough roses.

Made in 2000, *To Have and To Hold* is vinyl with hard-plastic bendable legs. ဆ

Dazzling Duos

lthough husbands and wives are equal partners in life, the groom definitely plays a supporting role on the wedding day. Everyone, even passersby, turns to see the star—the bride. Dollmakers, too, are guilty of playing favorites; even the largest producers of bride dolls have offered just a handful of grooms. *To Have and To Hold*, a couple captured in a loving embrace by Stephanie Blythe, is one of those rare pieces that captures the beauty of both bride *and* groom.

Second in a series of figures that depict lovers from different periods in time, this wonderful wedding duo wear romantic, late-medieval-inspired clothing. The artist chose to dress both bride and groom in white, creating contrast in the garments by using fabric of varying textures. Girded with golden chains, the bride's gown has an underskirt fashioned from a piece of sheer embroidered silk from a real eighteenth-century gown. The bride's overdress is patterned silk, as is her long cloak, which is accented at the shoulders with handmade lace dotted with tiny pearls. Her sleeves are antique metallic mesh over silk. On top of her long golden locks, a gold-washed sterling circlet anchors the antique lace-edged silk net veil.

The groom's costume is made of layers of patterned silk, ribbon, and white and gold trim. The ensemble includes a silk shirt, a jacket of embroidered silk and brocade, silk hose, and white leather boots. On his head he wears a ornamental fillet, or band, of antique brass.

The creation of each stunning work in Blythe's Lovers series is time-consuming and fraught with technical challenges that only a master artist could overcome. Each duo is cast from nine separate, multi-part molds made from Blythe's original sculpture. The cast figures are then combined, fitted and re-sculpted together, and fired as one piece. Costuming the assembled duo is equally daunting: the garments must be sewn, then cut apart in order to fit around the intertwined pair, and, finally, re-stitched together.

Like all the pieces in the Lovers series, *To Have and To Hold* is a one-of-a-kind interpretation with unique costuming, painting, and hair. The bride's wig is made from raw silk; the groom's locks are hand-dyed Tibetan lambswool. &

To Have and To Hold,
10 inches, porcelain, 1999

Victorian Bride and Groom, 17 and 16½ inches, polyform clay and cloth, 2000

S
ome late nineteenth-century brides wed in their "going-away" dress, as demonstrated by this practical Victorian lady. Created by Betsey Baker, she wears a long basque of moiré taffeta with a high-necked lace collar and lace cuffs. The bustled skirt has a center panel of hand-dyed and shirred lace and two ruffles of pleated satin at the hem. The gown is embellished throughout with braided trim. On her head the bride wears a tulle veil trimmed with lace and fabric flowers; in her hand is a kid-leather-covered bible. Her *Victorian Groom* wears a black wool afternoon coat lined with cotton, a white

silk shirt, a blue satin waistcoat, and gray wool pants. A top hat of black wool and a pair of gray kid-leather gloves complete his ensemble. "I wanted to capture the pair right after the ceremony, as they start their life together," says Baker, who has been making dolls more than thirty years. The *Victorian Bride and Groom* are one-of-a-kind and have polyform clay heads, arms, and legs. Their bodies are cloth over wire. ❧

Jackie and John, 10 inches, hard
plastic, 1996
Inset: Mr. and Mrs. John F. Kennedy

In 1996, the Alexander Doll Company commemorated the September 12, 1953, wedding of Jacqueline Lee Bouvier and John Fitzgerald Kennedy with this charming duo. Inspired by Mrs. Kennedy's breathtaking real-life bridal ensemble, the *Jackie* doll wears an ivory taffeta gown with a portrait neckline. On the sleeveless bodice, bands of pleated satin reach from bustline to waist. The full skirt is adorned with large satin ribbon rosebuds; five rows of satin ribbon decorate the hem. Completing the ensemble are a strand of faux pearls, a train-length veil of embroidered lace, a pair of gloves, and a bouquet of pastel fabric blossoms. The handsome groom wears a tail coat and wool pinstripe pants, white shirt, gray vest with faux pearl buttons, and a satin tie. *Jackie and John* are hard plastic with sleep eyes. ଔ

pretend wedding can be as fun as a real one; the only problem is, the clothes don't fit! Looking a little lost in their parents' wedding finery, *Jenni and Jeffy* play bride and groom. *Jeffy* is a gent in a cotton tuxedo with bow tie, top hat, and Dad's best shoes; *Jenni* is princess-pretty in a lace-trimmed eyelet dress, tulle veil, and white cotton bloomers. The bride has also borrowed Mom's high heels and pearl necklace. Part of the Daddy's Long Legs collection, *Jenni and Jeffy* were offered in 1998 only and commemorated the wedding of Karen and Brent Germany's son and daughter-in-law. The dolls have resin heads, resin bodies, and resin lower limbs; the upper limbs are cloth. Accompanying *Jenni and Jeffy* is Boo the Flower Puppy (a tribute to one of the Germanys' beloved Yorkshire terriers), a gift to members of the Daddy's Long Legs Collectors Club in 1998. ❧

Jenni and Jeffy, 12½ and 13 inches, resin and fabric, 1998

Bride & Groom Set, 8 inches, hard plastic, 1997

Neat, sweet, and petite, Ginny dresses up as *The Blushing Bride* for a pretend wedding. Designed by Wendy Lawton, the snow-white bridal gown is tissue taffeta. A flounce at the hem is caught up with satin rosettes, revealing a lacy underskirt; a lace appliqué and a satin rosette accent the bodice. Ginny also wears a fingertip-length lace veil (satin rosettes adorn the headpiece), a powder-blue satin ribbon garter (no peeking!), and white slippers. She carries a posy of satin roses. Part of Vogue's Here Comes the Bride collection,

The Blushing Bride was sold alone and in a *Bride & Groom Set*. Dapper in a tuxedo with tails, crisp white shirt, blue satin cummerbund with matching bow tie, boutonniere, and top hat, Ginny also makes a darling groom.

Made of hard plastic with sleep eyes, the couple debuted in 1997. A matching *Maid of Honor* Ginny (see page 88) debuted the same year. ❧

We can find true love at any age, as Annie Wahl demonstrates with her mature matrimonial duo. A tribute to couples who fall in love later in life, *Second Time Around* reflects the artist's forte for creating warm, lighthearted characters. Most of her dolls depict elderly people—wrinkles, crinkles, and all. "I never compete with beauty," Wahl says of her work.

Made for debut in *Here Come the Bride Dolls*, *Second Time Around* is a one-of-a-kind sculpture. The bride and groom donned their Sunday Best for their wedding, which was a quiet affair, the artist says. "He had a suit and it was a pretty good suit, so he wore that. She probably got her dress out of a JCPenney catalog—polyester, you know! Maybe she could wear it again...." The modest matron jazzed up her ensemble with a sparkly polyester jacket; she also wears a crocheted hat with attached veil. "For these dolls, the costuming was not as important as the emotion and expression," the artist points out. Both bride and groom have a sculpted polyform clay head, polyform clay arms and legs, and poseable, cloth-over-wire bodies. Their eyes are glass beads.

A former art student at the University of Minnesota, Wahl "got serious about making dolls" in 1985, when she began working with polyform clay (previously, she'd made dolls out of cornhusk, batik, and other materials). In addition to creating one-of-a-kind sculptures, she designs characters for the Collection of the Masters by Richard Simmons doll line, which is produced by Goebel of Pennington, New Jersey. "Richard started buying my dolls because he felt that they represented the big family that he'd never had and always wanted," says the artist, the youngest of six children.

The dollmaker found true love herself at the tender age of twenty-one. She married Tom Wahl on September 2, 1972. The Wahls have two children and live happily ever after in Lakeville, Minnesota. ✤

Second Time Around,
11 inches, polyform clay, 2000
Inset: Annie and Tom Wahl
September 2, 1972

This handsome couple took their vows in 1999, courtesy of the Robert Tonner Doll Company. *Felicity* is radiant in a gown of silk shantung embroidered with sequins and clusters of faux pearls. The ensemble also includes elbow-length gloves, a faux pearl necklace, and a floor-length tulle veil. *Eric*, the handsome groom, is the first vinyl male fashion figure designed by Tonner. "Since I'd made so many brides, *Eric* had to debut in a tuxedo!" Tonner jokes. *Eric*'s lined, wool tuxedo jacket has a satin shawl collar and angled satin pocket flaps; the pleated wool pants have a satin stripe down either side. The groom also wears a tucked cotton shirt with black stud buttons and black cuff links, a satin bow tie and cummerbund, and leather shoes. (A honeymoon secret: underneath *Eric*'s elegant ensemble is a pair of heart-printed boxers!) Part of Tonner's American Model Collection, each vinyl doll was issued in an edition of 500. &

Felicity Bride and Eric,
19 and 21 inches, vinyl, 1999

When Caroline and Franck Fonteneau wed in Nantes, France, on June 22, 1991, they received a unique gift: a pair of bride and groom dolls made by well-known French artist Héloïse. What makes these dolls even more precious is that they represent the bride and groom in miniature form. The figures were not sculpted as portraits; rather, they are one-of-a-kind versions of two of the artist's limited-edition dolls that have been painted, wigged, and costumed to look like the Fonteneaus.

The dolls' exquisitely rendered garments were made by Danielle Pallac, the seamstress who helps Héloïse costume her creations. The expert needlewoman also happens to be the mother of Caroline Fonteneau, and the maker of her lovely gown! For the bride and the doll, Pallac created a shirred-silk sheath that ends at the knees. A cloud of tulle extends from the hem to the floor, forming a wide train. The sleeves (cap on the bride; just past the elbow on the doll) are trimmed at the shoulders with rosettes. A short tulle veil attached to a headpiece of fabric flowers completes the ensemble. Like the real groom, *Franck* is dressed in a stylish suit of light brown wool. His dashing ensemble includes a satin cummerbund, a matching bow tie, and two-tone shoes.

Héloïse, whose real name is Joëlle Lemasson, began making dolls in 1976, using cloth. She began working with resin, her medium of choice, in 1982. *Caroline and Franck*, which are one-of-a-kind versions of the dolls *Anne Sophie* and *Hugo* (introduced in 1988), have sculpted resin heads and resin arms and legs. Their bodies are cloth; wigs are mohair. Like all of Héloïse's creations, they are beautifully handpainted with luminous eyes, an effect achieved by painting the eyes with watercolors, then touching them with a drop of translucent resin. ಜ

Above: Caroline and Franck
Fonteneau, June 22, 1991

*Caroline and Franck, 18 inches,
resin and cloth, 1991*

*A*nd now, ladies and gentlemen, let's welcome the newly-weds, dancing their first dance as Mr. and Mrs.... *Frankenstein?"*

Not your typical wedding couple, the Frankenstein monster and his bride give new meaning to the phrase "till death do us part." The groom is appropriately attired in tattered tails adorned with a daisy boutonniere. His suit is flocked nylon; his vest is cotton. The bride's gown is metallic gold fabric with an overlayer of ivory lace; the ribbons simulate bandages. With her scarred face and towering Elsa Lanchester hair-do, Mrs. F. is the epitome of graveyard glamour.

Inspired in part by the classic 1935 horror film *The Bride of Frankenstein* and other old horror films, *Mr. and Mrs. Frankenstein* were produced by the Alexander Doll Company in 1996. The duo are made of hard plastic and have sleep eyes. These lovebirds clearly can't get enough of each other: They are handcuffed together for eternity. ✴

Mr. and Mrs. Frankenstein, 8 inches, hard plastic, 1996

idge is one sidekick who wasn't always the bridesmaid: In 1991, this devoted friend of Barbie wed long-time love, Alan. At the American International Toy Fair that year, Mattel celebrated the couple's nuptials by giving away pretend wedding day memorabilia, including match books, napkins, and a mock newspaper article announcing the marriage. Dainty and demure, the bride's dotted swiss dress is trimmed with lace. Her ensemble includes long, lacy fingerless gloves, a fingertip-length tulle veil, a garter, and a bouquet of roses. (The gown is practical, too: the skirt is removable, leaving a short dress that becomes a "going away" outfit when combined with a jacket that came with the doll.) The groom is equally elegant in a tuxedo jacket, jumpsuit, vest, and ascot. *Wedding Day Midge* and *Wedding Day Alan* were sold separately and were also available in a *Wedding Party Gift Set* that included Barbie as a bridesmaid, Ken as best man, flower girl Kelly, and ring bearer Todd. ๛

Wedding Party Gift Set, 12 inches,
11½ inches and 8 inches, vinyl, 1991

This cozy couple braved winter winds to wed in early January, during the celebration of Kwanzaa. Created by Anne Myatt, this bride and groom have chosen to incorporate many elements of their African-American heritage into their ceremony and garments. "That was one of my goals when I made this piece," the artist says.

Made of taffeta, the bride's sheath-style gown has an Empire waistline, long lace sleeves, and a detachable train. The dress is accented throughout with gold and white lace trims and appliqués. A bit of tulle veiling flows from an elaborate headpiece that accentuates the bride's braided hair. Made of taffeta, the headpiece was inspired by African bridal wear and is embellished with golden beads and trim. The ensemble includes a beaded necklace and shoes of taffeta and lace.

The groom's ensemble has a strong African influence, Myatt says. His long tunic is fashioned of paisley print brocade. It's paired with pants of white grosgrain rayon. On his head he wears a *gelee*, or beret, of the same fabric as the tunic. The groom also wears leather shoes.

Myatt explains that the couple's broom harks back to the pre-Civil War era, when slaves could not legally marry. In lieu of an official ceremony, the bride and groom were permitted to acknowledge their relationship by jumping over a broom. In her book *Happy Is the Bride the Sun Shines On: Wedding Beliefs, Customs, and Traditions* (Contemporary Books, 1995), author Leslie Jones describes the ritual:

The man laid the broom on the floor with the brush facing north, took his bride by the hand, and the two stepped over the broom and back again. Then the bride placed the broom with the brush toward the south and they repeated the process. This was supposed to keep away bad luck and evil spirits through their lives.

"Nowadays, many young African-American couples are including the 'jumping the broom' tradition in their wedding ceremony. If I could do it over again, I would, too!" says the artist, who wed Al Myatt in 1971.

Second in the artist's Bridal Seasons series, the *Kwanzaa Couple* are one-of-a-kind. The doll's heads are cloth over polyform clay; their bodies, arms and legs are cloth with an armature of wire and wood. Their expressive eyes are polyform clay handpainted with acrylics by the artist. ☙

Kwanzaa Couple, 17 and
18 inches, mixed media, 2000
Inset: Anne and Al Myatt
October 16, 1971

Always a Bridesmaid

Bridesmaids, not diamonds, are a girl's best friend. Who else can you count on to help write out place cards, run a last-minute errand, and pin up your train? At one time, bridesmaids even served as body guards, of sorts: dressed similarly to the bride, the attendants would supposedly confuse any evil spirits who happened to be lurking about on the wedding day. (And you thought planning a shower was hard work!) Many dollmakers have chosen to pay tribute to these most faithful of friends who, despite all their labors, will probably never get to wear that dress again....

In their own celebration of friendship, Paul Crees and Peter Coe joined forces with fellow artist Linda Mason in 1997 to create the charming *Buttercup Bridesmaid*. "This was a fun collaboration," Mason says. "Peter and Paul love to make brides, so a little bridesmaid seemed like the right choice." Mason, who makes her home in California, spent two weeks with Crees and Coe in their studio in England. She created the original sculpture for *Buttercup*, and all three artists brainstormed on her costume.

The lovely little lady wears a cream silk embroidered gown tied at the waist with a sash of gold dupioni silk. The sash is trimmed with cream and yellow satin roses, as is her upswept auburn hair. A contemporary creation with traditional roots, the gown has pearl-trimmed leg-of-mutton sleeves that end in points and a full, bell-shaped skirt.

When *Buttercup* was finished, the artists realized that the youngster would be lonely without a companion, hence the creation of the *Buttercup Bride*. Sculpted by Crees and Coe, the statuesque lady wears a gown similar in design to the dress worn by her doting attendant. Her ensemble includes a train-length silk tulle veil and a posy of cream roses nestled in lace.

The bride is made entirely of wax; the bridesmaid has a wax head, wax arms and legs, and a cloth body. The dolls have handpainted eyes and were each limited to an edition of fifteen. ❧

When Mel Odom created Gene, he gave her a richly detailed life story that recalls the glory days of Hollywood, when leading ladies were always beautiful, poised, and classy. Born Katie Gene Marshall in Cos Cob, Connecticut, in 1923, Gene sought fame and fortune in New York City. While working as a theater usherette, she was discovered by big-name Hollywood director "Eric Von Sternberg" (Odom's homage to real-life directors Josef von Sternberg and Erich von Stroheim), who cast her in his next film. When the film's star was felled by a freak accident ("there were trap doors all over the set for a musical number called 'You Floor Me,' and she fell through one of them," Odom explains matter-of-factly), Gene's bit part was beefed up to a major role, and she became an instant star.

By the early 1950s, Gene is a Hollywood powerhouse. But a hometown girl at heart, she returns to Cos Cob to keep a promise made years before: to serve as maid of honor at a dear friend's wedding. A never-before-published prototype Gene fashion, *Younger Than Springtime* is a circa-1951 pink organza bridesmaid dress lined in pale-pink satin. A garland of bright pink chiffon flower petals edges the strapless bodice and wraps around the single short sleeve. The full skirt is dramatically accented with pink chiffon flower petals dotted with faux pearls. Designed by Christine Curtis, a graduate of New York City's Traphagen School of Design and Illustration, *Younger Than Springtime* includes a flower-trimmed headpiece, long pale-pink gloves, a pink tulle crinoline, hose, and pink high heels.

When Gene arrives in Cos Cob, everyone is excited to see the town's famous former resident. But gracious Gene keeps a low profile, ensuring that the bride is the star of the day. She could have gotten a few pointers from Anna Petro (née Deliman), the author's mother-in-law, who served as a junior bridesmaid once and a bridesmaid six times from the late 1940s through the 1950s. When she was just fifteen, Anna donned a strapless gown similar in style to Gene's for the 1952 wedding of family friend Maria Sabak and Joseph Fedorczyk. (In the photo, above, she is the first bridesmaid on the left.) Anna's turquoise taffeta gown was topped with a sheer bolero jacket—a must for a church wedding!

Only three prototypes of Gene in *Younger Than Springtime* were ever made. ✌

Above: The 1952 wedding party of Maria Sabak and Joseph Fedorczyk
Opposite page: Younger Than Springtime, *15½ inches, vinyl, 1999*

Left: Maid of Honor, 8 inches, hard plastic, 1997
Below: Bride Laura Sipko with her pretty-in-pink sisters, October 26, 1991
Opposite page: Kaylie Bridesmaid, 18 inches, vinyl, 1995

Although pink is just one of many popular colors for bridesmaid dresses, it's probably the one most people think of first when they hear the word bridesmaid. Kaylie, (shown on the opposite page) the first doll costumed as a bridesmaid by the Robert Tonner Doll Company, is a proud member of the pretty-in-pink club. Her short-sleeved, rose-pink dress and matching slippers are made of rayon moiré. The bodice is accented with an organza collar and a sash at the waist. The skirt is drawn up at the hem (fabric flowers trim the gathers), revealing an organza-trimmed underskirt. Pink fabric flowers are the perfect decoration for Kaylie's shimmering tresses.

Kaylie has the distinction of being the first vinyl doll produced by the Robert Tonner Doll Company. Representing a girl of about ten years of age, she debuted in 1993. The *Kaylie Bridesmaid* was introduced in 1995 in an edition of 500 and has painted eyes.

One of the most famous dolls of all time, Ginny, too, donned pink for her turn as a bridal attendant. Part of Vogue's Here Comes the Bride collection, Ginny as the *Maid of Honor* debuted in 1997. Her yummy sherbet-pink gown, designed by Wendy Lawton, has many of the same stylistic elements as the gown worn by *The Blushing Bride* (see page 75), who debuted the same year. Ginny's dress is organdy with short pouffed sleeves. The skirt is trimmed at the hem with a ruffle that's caught up with silk rosettes, revealing a lace underskirt. *Maid of Honor* wears a picture hat trimmed at the back with a large tulle bow and underneath the brim with pleated organdy and a satin rosette. Made of hard plastic with sleep eyes, she carries a posy of pink and white satin roses.

For her October 26, 1991, wedding, real-life bride Laura Sipko picked pink for her bridesmaids, sisters Vivian Dabrowski and Annette Minolfo. In true sisterly fashion, each bridesmaid found a way to personalize her dress: Vivian wore the wide collar above her shoulders, while Annette (the rebellious one) preferred an off-the-shoulder look. ❧

Just like a real flower girl, this little beauty holds a bouquet of fresh flowers; her hair is also decorated with real blooms. "I wanted to create a fleeting moment," says her creator, Joanne Callander. "I've always designed dolls with their possible future value foremost in my mind. With this piece, I wanted to go the other extreme and create work that was fresh as a daisy, but, like a daisy, would last only for a day."

To her dismay, Callander discovered that her unique creation lasted even less than a day: as she struggled to photograph the doll, the flowers drooped and withered under the hot lights. Hence the doll as she appears here no longer exists—truly a one-of-a-kind!

A dainty six inches tall, the *Real Flower Flower Girl* was made to debut in *Here Come the Bride Dolls*. She wears a draped and tucked gown of off-white silk chiffon accented at the neckline with a ruffle of pink nylon and at the waist with a cummerbund of pale-pink china silk. Her beautiful cascading bouquet and wreath-like headpiece are blends of penny royal, baby's breath, pink sedum, and yellow yarrow. (Callander, who

lives on a family farm in California's wine country, picked most of the flowers from her own well-tended garden.) "For the greenery, I used asparagus sprouts—hold the hollandaise!" the artist says with a laugh.

The *Real Flower Flower Girl* is porcelain from head to toe and is a one-of-a-kind version of *Pistachio*, one of Callander's limited-edition dolls. Her eyes are sculpted of polyform clay, then covered with resin; her plaited hairdo is mohair.

Although the *Real Flower Flower Girl* is Callander's first (and probably last!) piece embellished with blossoms, the artist is well-known for costuming her dolls in unexpected ways. Using vintage fabrics and trimmings as well as beads and baubles, she deftly concocts ensembles that please the eye and stir the imagination. As ethereal as she is lovely, the *Real Flower Flower Girl* is Callander's first wedding-themed creation. ❧

*Real Flower Flower Girl,
6 inches, porcelain, 2000*

ronically, the idea for these innocent young lovelies was born in the Stanley Hotel in Estes Park, Colorado, the same locale that inspired Stephen King's horror novel *The Shining*. Helen Kish, the dolls' creator, recalls, "My husband and I took some out-of-town guests to the historic hotel. While we wandered through the large lobby, we happened upon a wedding about to take place. There was a little flower girl in the most charming gown. None of us had a camera, so I attempted to commit the detail of her gown to my memory. That one child became two dolls wearing pleated silk gowns with lace slips."

Each limited to an edition of 35, auburn-haired *Emilie*, the bridesmaid, and fair *Juliette*, the flower girl, are made of porcelain. The expressive eyes are handpainted by the artist; the prettily styled wigs are mohair. Both gowns have Empire waists, short pouffed sleeves, and end in points at front and back. *Emilie*'s waist is tied with a satin sash; *Juliette*'s bodice is lightly embellished with silk-ribbon embroidered roses. Ladylike from head to toe, each girl wears white leather shoes and white tights.

Although Helen Kish is best known for her porcelain and vinyl dolls of sweet-faced children with beestung lips, her commanding repertoire includes breathtaking, often enigmatic art pieces executed in stoneware, bronze, porcelain, and other media. A native of Denver, Colorado, Kish majored in art at the University of Colorado and studied anatomy and life drawing at the Rocky Mountain School of Art. She began making dolls in the mid 1970s, concentrating on sculpting young girls. "I find children very beautiful," she told the author for a 1988 cover story in *Dolls* magazine. ✇

Not all bridesmaids are happy with their lot, as Nancy Walters illustrates with this gawky teen. Everything is going wrong: her dress doesn't quite fit (it's too roomy in the bust, the universal bridesmaid's nightmare); her shoes hurt; her stockings are bagging. "I think she is the sister of the bride, otherwise she would never have agreed to do it," says Walters, who often infuses her pieces with humor. Made in 1993, *Always a Bridesmaid* caught the eye of another clever lady, Lynn Johnston. The creator of the *For Better or For Worse* comic strip, Johnston knew that this doll belonged in her collection. "*Always a Bridesmaid* is like a novella," she says. "When you look at this obviously desperate-feeling young woman, you know she's thinking, 'let me please survive this day!'" *Always a Bridesmaid* has a sculpted porcelain clay head, sculpted porcelain clay arms and legs, and a cloth body with a wire armature. The despised dress is taffeta trimmed with lace. The one-of-a-kind doll was intended as the first piece in a series depicting adolescents going through what Walters calls "devastating" experiences: "things that we thought would shatter us for the rest of our lives, like a run in our stocking on a big date." ❧

Always a Bridesmaid, 19 inches, porcelain and cloth, 1993

Little Yolanda, 14 inches, porcelain and cloth, 1995
Inset: Yolanda Bello as an irresistible three-year-old flower girl

If anyone can steal the show from the bride, it's the flower girl. Cherubic, charming, and often adorably confused, she is simply irresistible. In 1995, the Ashton-Drake Galleries introduced *Little Yolanda*, a self-portrait of Venezuelan-born artist Yolanda Bello when she was a three-year-old flower girl at a cousin's wedding. The blonde-haired, blue-eyed cutie wears a white organza dress with an embroidered overskirt. The bodice has short pouffed sleeves and is embellished with beaded appliqués. Fabric flowers are sprinkled in her hair. The doll's head, arms, and legs are porcelain; her body is cloth. *Little Yolanda* came with a reproduction of Yolanda Bello's childhood photo and was retired in 1996.

Dolls that depict toddlers have long been a specialty for Bello, who began sculpting in the early 1980s. "All people react to my work the same way: They say a doll reminds them of their child or their childhood," she told the author for a 1989 cover story in *Dolls* magazine. ◈

Seven-year-old bridesmaid Anna Goddu in 1995
Opposite page: Eliza, 32 inches, porcelain and cloth, 2000

For their lovely young bridesmaid, *Eliza*, the husband-and-wife team of Zofia and Henry Zawierusynski passed on pastels, opting instead for pure white. (During the Victorian era, white was the color of choice for both brides and bridesmaids.) An imaginative confection of silk and lace, *Eliza*'s costume is contemporary yet romantic. The gown's bodice, made of lace over silk, has an Empire waist and short sleeves. The off-the-shoulder neckline is beautifully accented with ecru satiny cord intertwined with fabric leaves and dainty clay flowers in white and pink. The silk skirt splits in front, revealing an underskirt of lace. The bridesmaid's sandals are porcelain with lace straps. Her bouquet and headpiece are made of the same clay flowers that adorn her dress; a single bloom accents *Eliza*'s choker. Limited to an edition of five, the *Eliza* bridesmaid was made for debut in *Here Come the Bride Dolls*. She has a porcelain head and shoulder plate, porcelain arms and legs, and a cloth body with a wire armature. Her wig is made of human hair.

Coincidentally, *Eliza* bears some resemblance to real-life bridesmaid Anna Goddu (daughter of Krystyna Poray Goddu, the editor of this book), who donned white for an outdoor Connecticut wedding in 1995. Then seven years old, Anna wore a dainty handmade dress of swiss eyelet with net trim and short pouffed net sleeves. Anna's mom explains that the dress was originally made for her first holy communion: "Anna wanted a dress with a 'cupcake' skirt, meaning that when she whirled around and knelt down, the skirt made a cupcake shape on the floor." For the communion ceremony, the dress's hem and sleeve cuffs were threaded with white ribbon. For the wedding, the white ribbon was replaced with teal, the color of the maid-of-honor's dress.

Besides having a white bridesmaid's dress in common, Anna Goddu and *Eliza* also share a Polish ancestry. Anna's maternal grandparents were born and raised in Poland, as were *Eliza*'s "parents," the Zawierusynkis. Zofia was born in Niska, a small city in southeast Poland; Henry was born in Szczecin, a city on the Baltic Sea. Married in 1971, the couple ran a successful interior design business before emigrating to the United States in 1988. ✤

Canadian artist Heather Maciak, who studied fashion design at North Texas State University, created a special piece for *Here Come the Bride Dolls*: a flower girl whose costume complements the ensembles worn by the bridal attendants at the author's October 20, 1996, wedding. Referring to a photo of one of the silk bridesmaid dresses (a Laura Ashley design with a delicate floral pattern), Maciak combed fabric shops, searching for material that would coordinate with the full-size garment yet still be in proper scale for a small-size doll. All the floral patterns she found were too large, so she improvised: Using a silvery-blue cotton as a background, she embroidered an all-over pattern of dainty violet blossoms, thus creating her own fabric. To this she added a white, bib-shaped collar embellished with embroidered sprays of lavender and violet flowers, tiny beads, and lavender silk ribbon. Touches of lavender highlight the ensemble throughout: lavender cotton for the sleeve cuffs and the skirt hem; lavender silk ribbon shoe ties; a lavender hair ribbon.

Named *Logan*, the fresh-faced flower girl is made of porcelain. She has a fully poseable, ball-jointed body and handpainted eyes. While some artists strive to make dolls that mimic the expressions of real children, Maciak prefers a stylized look that "captures the softness" found in every child. Poised, perky, and free of froufrou, her youngsters bring to mind the mouth-watering aroma of home-baked bread and the familiar warmth of an old handmade patchwork quilt.

Logan would have made a perfect flower girl for the author's wedding, which was celebrated at Crabtree's Kittle House (a historic inn and restaurant) in Chappaqua, New York. You can almost imagine the chestnut-haired cutie joining this portrait of the bride and her attendants: bridesmaids Maria Saldana and Lynn Amos (left and right, respectively) and maid of honor Ellen Fecher.

Logan is limited to an edition of ten, but only five wear the flower girl ensemble, which includes a basket of silky blooms. ✍

Above: The author with attendants Maria Saldana, Ellen Fecher, and Lynn Amos, October 20, 1996
Opposite page: Logan, 10½ inches, porcelain, 2000

Commemorative Gowns

On September 12, 1953, one of the most elegant brides in United States history walked down the aisle of St. Mary's Roman Catholic church in Newport, Rhode Island. The bride, of course, was Jacqueline Lee Bouvier, and her handsome groom was John Fitzgerald Kennedy, the young senator from Massachusetts. More than 750 guests attended the ceremony; outside, 3,000 well-wishers waited to greet the happy young couple. A work of art rendered in silk taffeta rather than oils, Jacqueline Bouvier's gown was made by Ann Lowe, an Alabama-born dressmaker. The shimmering dress featured a portrait neckline, an intricately tucked bodice, and a bouffant skirt embellished with large rosettes. The gown required fifty yards of fabric and took more than two months to construct.

The bride's veil, made of delicate rose point lace, was a family heirloom. It was secured with a tiara of lace and orange blossoms. Jacqueline Bouvier also wore a pearl necklace (another heirloom), a diamond bracelet (her wedding gift from her groom), a diamond pin shaped like a leaf (a gift from Ambassador and Mrs. Joseph P. Kennedy), and wrist-length gloves.

In 1996, The Franklin Mint issued an impressive porcelain portrait of the First Lady in her wedding attire. The doll captures the magic of this unique bridal gown as well as the timeless beauty of the woman who wore it. The gown is taffeta with hand-applied rosettes; the veil is a blend of rose point and point d'esprit laces. Replicas of two pieces of Jacqueline Bouvier's wedding jewelry are included in the ensemble: a gold-plated rhinestone bracelet and a necklace of faux pearls. The doll has a porcelain head, a porcelain chest plate, porcelain arms and legs, and a cloth body; the eyes are painted.

In their introduction to the catalog for Sotheby's April 1996 sale of the estate of Jacqueline Kennedy Onassis, Caroline B. Kennedy and the late John F. Kennedy, Jr., wrote that, for their mother, "history came alive through objects and paintings, as well as books." A part of our history certainly lives on in dolls like this one and many of the other figures shown in this chapter, which wear miniature replicas of some of the most famous wedding gowns ever worn. &

Newlyweds Mr. and Mrs. John F. Kennedy at Hammersmith Farm, site of their reception

Left: Artist C. Bunnell's drawing of Mrs. Grover Cleveland receiving a kiss from her mother, shown on the cover of Frank Leslie's Illustrated Newspaper
Below: Marriage of President Grover Cleveland and Frances Folsom, as drawn by artist Thure de Thulstrup for Harper's Weekly *in 1886*

Since 1812, when a sister of First Lady Dolley Madison wed at the White House, the mansion at 1600 Pennsylvania Avenue has hosted many celebrated weddings. Only once, however, have a President and First Lady-to-be tied the knot there. The date was June 2, 1886, and the bride and groom were Frances Folsom and President Grover Cleveland.

In 1995, the Alexander Doll Company created a *Frances Folsom* doll as a souvenir for the Madame Alexander Doll Club's convention in Arlington, Virginia. The idea for the event's theme ("A White House Wedding") and souvenir came from doll enthusiast and convention co-chair Phyllis West. "I wanted a doll that would represent someone outstanding, someone who had been the first to do something," she says. "Not only was Frances Folsom the first First Lady to be married in the White House; she was also the first First Lady to bear a child there."

The *Paris Morning News* described Frances Folsom's long-trained, ivory satin wedding gown as "a poem in its pure simplicity." The dress was accented with soft folds of silk India muslin at the front of the bodice and on one side of the skirt. Both bodice and skirt were outlined with a narrow band of orange blossoms and leaves; the sleeves were similarly trimmed. The bride wore a silk tulle veil—over six yards long!—which was secured atop her upswept hairdo with a crown of myrtle and orange blossoms.

The petite *Frances Folsom* doll—she's just ten inches tall—wears a miniature version of the First Lady's ensemble. The dress is made of satin with chiffon and net taking the place of the muslin. Fabric orange blossoms and green ribbon trim the gown; fabric flowers also make up the headpiece. The hard-plastic doll wears one long glove on her left hand and carries the other, just as Frances Folsom did during her wedding ceremony.

Brides-to-be whose fiancés are reluctant to help with wedding planning might like to know that President Cleveland himself organized his wedding, putting the White House head gardener in charge of flowers and asking composer/conductor John Philip Sousa to arrange the music. According to Marie Smith and Louise Durbin, authors of *White House Brides* (Acropolis Books, 1966), the President also struck the word "obey" from his wife's vows. ❧

*Frances Folsom, 10 inches,
hard plastic, 1995
Inset: Frances Folsom
in her wedding gown*

*Left and opposite page: Princess Diana, 28 inches, wax, 1998
Below: Prince Charles and Princess Diana on the balcony of Buckingham Palace after their wedding*

Glued to television sets in seventy countries, more than 750 million people were enthralled by the July 29, 1981, wedding of Lady Diana Spencer and Prince Charles. Just as Princess Diana's tragic death on August 31, 1997, sent a shock wave of grief through the world, her wedding offered the world a vision of happiness and hope. When this lovely and dignified young woman tripped over her vows, she won our hearts forever.

Few contemporary celebrities have been immortalized as a doll more often than Princess Diana. Most of these tributes depict the princess in her world-famous wedding gown, which was created by designers David and Elizabeth Emanuel. The most spectacular rendition of Princess Diana as a bride is this handmade wax version created by Paul Crees and Peter Coe, who faithfully reproduced every detail of the young bride's wonderful dress.

The *Princess Diana* doll is garbed in silk dupioni. The bodice has pouffed sleeves gathered into ruffles below the elbow and tied with silk bows. The neckline is embellished with a silk ruffle, a lace ruffle oversewn with faux pearls and sequins, and a silk bow. Lavishly beaded lace also trims the front of the bodice, the sleeve cuffs, and the edge of the full skirt and its ten-foot train. (The twenty-five-foot train of the real gown barely fit into the carriage that took the bride to St. Paul's Cathedral.) Flowing from a sparkling tiara, the veil is dusted with iridescent sequins. The finishing touch is a bouquet of white and cream silk flowers and silk ivy.

The *Princess Diana* doll was produced in 1998 in an edition of five. The piece is made of wax and is handpainted by Crees. "Princess Diana was a beauty in the 'English Rose' tradition, which of course inspired us to try and capture her in wax," he says. ❧

FATHER OF THE BRIDE AND ALL RELATED CHARACTERS AND ELEMENTS ARE TRADE-
MARKS OF TURNER ENTERTAINMENT CO. ©2001.

*H*elen Rose, two-time Oscar winner and seven-time nominee for best costume design, created two of the most famous bridal gowns of the 1950s: the gown worn by Grace Kelly when she wed Prince Rainier III of Monaco on April 19, 1956, and the gown worn by fictional bride Kay Banks, played by Elizabeth Taylor in the 1950 film *Father of the Bride.*

Based on the Edward Streeter novel, *Father of the Bride* stars Spencer Tracy as the harried Stanley T. Banks, whose daughter's "simple wedding" turns into his worst nightmare: a pull-out-all-the-stops event that costs a whopping *$3.75* a head! When he sees his lovely daughter in her wedding gown, however, he forgets all about the pile of bills. "She looked like the princess in a fairy tale," he says in awe.

Introduced by Mattel in 2000, the *Elizabeth Taylor in Father of the Bride* doll faithfully recreates Helen Rose's design. The bodice is satin, with a lace collar and yoke. Also satin, the trained skirt splits in front in billowy folds, revealing a lace underskirt. The tulle veil is trimmed with scalloped lace and flows from a headpiece of fabric flowers. A striking likeness of the young Elizabeth Taylor, the violet-eyed doll celebrates the magic of this classic film and its beautiful young star.

According to James Spada, author of *Grace: The Secret Lives of a Princess* (Doubleday and Company, 1987), Grace Kelly's wedding gown, at a cost of $7,226, was the most expensive dress Helen Rose ever created. Twenty-five yards of silk taffeta and one hundred yards of silk net went into the making of the ensemble, along with antique rose point lace and thousands of pearls.

The Princess Grace Heirloom Bride Doll, introduced by The Franklin Mint in 1992, accurately depicts this sumptuous ensemble. The lace-over-satin bodice has a tucked satin cummerbund and long sleeves; the trained satin skirt is embellished at the back with satin bows and a lace godet. The ensemble also includes a floor-length lace-edged veil attached to a headpiece of lace and fabric flowers, and a petticoat adorned with blue bows. In her hands the doll holds a lace-covered missal.

Made of porcelain with a cloth torso, the Princess Grace bride was authorized by the Princess Grace Foundation, which was created in 1964 to support aspiring artists. Would Princess Grace have enjoyed this porcelain likeness? Probably so: According to James Spada, when the princess moved from America to Prince Rainier's 220-room palace in Monaco, she took her childhood dolls with her. ❧

The Princess Grace Heirloom Bride Doll, 17 inches, porcelain and cloth, 1992
Inset: Princess Grace at her wedding.
Opposite page: Elizabeth Taylor in Father of the Bride, 11½ inches, vinyl, 2000

*I*n 1999, Mattel's designers deftly recreated two award-winning daytime drama divas—Susan Lucci of ABC's *All My Children* and Deidre Hall of NBC's *Days of Our Lives*—as TV brides. Sculpted in the likenesses of the actresses, the dolls capture the sophistication and beauty of these women as well as the delicious details of their romantic gowns.

The second doll in Mattel's Daytime Drama Collection, which celebrates the stars of ABC's soaps, the *Erica Kane Champagne Lace Wedding* doll depicts Pine Valley's famous femme fatale on the occasion of her first (in 1993) marriage to tall, dark, handsome, *and* wealthy Dimitri Marick (played by Michael Nader). Her form-fitting, mermaid-style gown is made of white floral-patterned lace over champagne satin and has a detachable tulle train. Crystal beads adorn the bodice. Erica's fingertip-length veil of iridescent tulle falls from a lacy headpiece. The ensemble also includes a faux diamond ring, faux pearl earrings, and a bouquet of ivory fabric blooms.

The *Marlena Evans* doll commemorates the long-awaited wedding of dashing John Black (played by Drake Hogestyn) and the statuesque Dr. Evans. Marlena's sheath-style ice-blue satin gown has a separate train attached at the waist. A long detachable cape of tulle falls gracefully from the shoulders. The bodice is adorned with lace, silver sequins, and crystal beads; silver cord trims the neckline. The silvery hue is echoed at the skirt's hem with a ruffle of scalloped white-and-silver lace. The bride also wears crystal drop earrings and a beaded bracelet, and she carries a nosegay of white fabric flowers. ✂

Opposite page, far left: Erica Kane Champagne Lace
Wedding, 11½ inches, vinyl, 1999
Opposite page, left: Erica Kane at her 1993
wedding to Dimitri Marick
Above: Marlena Evans, 11½ inches, vinyl, 1999
Inset: Dr. Marlena Evans and her groom, John Black

Left: Margaret Woodbury Strong Bride,
13 inches, porcelain and cloth, 1982
Below: Margaret Woodbury and Homer
Strong, September 20, 1920

Margaret Woodbury Strong and Lee Middleton weren't royalty or movie stars, but to doll enthusiasts, they were leading ladies in their own right. Born in 1897, Margaret Woodbury Strong was the ultimate collector: Before her death in 1969, she had amassed an array of antique furniture and decorative objects, including an astounding 30,000 dolls! The Strong Museum in Rochester, New York—the permanent home of Mrs. Strong's collection—opened in 1982. That same year, it released a portrait doll of Margaret Woodbury Strong. Made by artist Jeanne Singer, the doll was modeled after a 1920 wedding portrait.

The *Margaret Woodbury Strong Bride* wears an ivory satin gown that reaches to just below the knee. The bodice has a bib-shaped overlay of lace and tulle, long net sleeves accented with vertical stitching, and a satin cummerbund. A narrow satin train falls from the shoulders. The skirt is covered with net and has a lace-trimmed net apron. The doll wears the long veil favored by 1920s brides. Made of net edged with lace, it falls from a Juliet cap trimmed with plastic orange blossoms. Limited to an edition of 100, the *Margaret Woodbury Strong Bride* has a porcelain head and chest plate, porcelain arms and legs, and a cloth body. Her bobbed hairdo, stockings, and pumps are part of the sculpture.

Lee Middleton began sculpting dolls in the late 1970s. In 1994, her Belpre, Ohio, company—Lee Middleton Original Dolls—introduced *The Bride*, a 36-inch porcelain doll wearing a gown patterned after the one that Lee Middleton wore for her October 2, 1993, marriage to Gerry Urick. (The wedding gown itself was designed and made by Middleton.) In 1995, the company released a smaller, vinyl version, this time wearing a pair of ruby slippers.

Lee Middleton's daughter, Brynn Riordan, tells the charming tale of the shoes: "The ruby slippers were an inside story between my mom and Gerry. My mother bought our eighty-three-acre farm in 1980. When Gerry first visited the farm, it was winter, and Mom kept telling him that in the spring it was just like Oz, because it was so green. When spring came, Gerry was amazed by the farm's beauty. Mom said it was Oz, and Gerry made her feel like Dorothy, only this Oz was home. So when they got married, Mom took a pair of red satin shoes and meticulously glued thousands of ruby-colored rhinestone to them. They weighed about eight pounds each, and that is what she wore under her gown."

The Bride, Ruby Slipper Edition wears a formal trained gown of ivory satin brocade with lace trim. Mauve roses trim the bustle and pouffed sleeves. The doll was limited to an edition of 1,000. Available separately was a book, *The Ruby Slippers*, written by Lee Middleton. The much-loved artist, who was especially known for her baby dolls, passed away in 1997. ଔ

The Bride, Ruby Slipper Edition, 20 inches, vinyl, 1995
Inset: Lee Middleton and Gerry Urick, October 2, 1993

Hitty Bride, 6 3/8 inches, wood, 1994

She's famous, she's a bride, and best of all, she's a real doll! She is, of course, the star of Rachel Field's *Hitty: Her First Hundred Years* (Macmillan, 1929), illustrated by Dorothy P. Lathrop. A winner of the American Library Association's John Newbery Medal (an annual award given to outstanding children's books), this book is treasured by generations of doll enthusiasts. The fictitious "memoirs" of Mehitabel (Hitty for short), a handcarved doll, the tale traces her adventures from her "birth" in rural Maine to her retirement to a New York City antiques shop. One stop along the 100-year journey is the home of two aged Southern belles, who lovingly dress Hitty as a bride in "some of the finest cotton ever woven or worked": their great-grandmother's wedding handkerchief.

Working in partnership with Don and Sandy Reinke of Classics in Wood, Mary Lee Sundstrom introduced her Story Doll series of handmade wooden dolls in 1992 with *Hitty*. Limited to an edition of 100, the 6 3/8-inch doll was sold

wearing either a calico dress and bonnet or in undergarments only. Sandy Reinke made about a dozen bridal outfits for *Hitty* as special orders, and costumed this *Hitty Bride* in 1994. "I wanted to see how close I could come to the bride picture in the book," she says. Reinke couldn't have come a hair closer; the bride is an exacting copy of the doll as she appears in Lathrop's illustration. The gown's bodice and two-tier sleeves are French lace. The skirt is pleated and hand-smocked, with a short overskirt of cotton and French lace accented with silk flowers. Hitty's headpiece is a wreath of handmade silk-ribbon roses; her veil is cotton tulle.

Now retired, Sundstrom, a former commercial artist, carved all of the prototype dolls for the Story Doll series. Don Reinke, a retired navy commander, replicated the wooden parts by machine, then gave the pieces to Sundstrom, who finished them by hand. Reinke jointed the dolls, Sundstrom painted them, and Sandy Reinke, a former home economics teacher,

Hitty as a bride, as illustrated by Dorothy P. Lathrop in Hitty: Her First Hundred Years

made the costumes.

The Sundstrom/Reinke Hittys are highly sought after by the doll's many fans. "Mary Lee captured the essence of Dorothy Lathrop's illustrations; when you see Mary Lee's Hitty for the first time, you think that the doll stepped right out of the pages of the book," says Virginia Ann Heyerdahl, founder of the Friends of Hitty Club and editor and publisher of the club's newsletter. "The Hitty dressed in Sandy's detailed bridal costume is considered one of the most desirable examples of this duo's fine work," Heyerdahl adds. ⁊

Literary Ladies

R omantic leading ladies from books, poems, fables, and fairy tales have inspired the creation of many bride dolls. For artist Lisa Lichtenfels, the tragic legend of Persephone was hard to resist. "She's a reluctant bride," the artist explains. According to Greek mythology, beautiful Persephone, daughter of Zeus and Demeter, caught the eye of Hades, who carried her off to the underworld. In mourning for her stolen daughter, Demeter, goddess of crops, let the earth turn barren. To restore life to earth, Zeus secured Persephone's release. But there was a catch: Because Persephone had eaten the seed of a pomegranate, a fruit sacred to the underworld, she had to return to Hades four months of each year. Persephone's annual return to the earth heralds the coming of spring.

A study in sadness, *Persephone* was a breakthrough work for Lichtenfels. "It was one of my first pieces that used compositional direction to tell the story," she explains. The positioning of the figure's arms and legs, and even the folds of her diaphanous gown (it's made from an antique bridal dress and veil), lead the eye downward. *Persephone*'s hands lie limp in her lap with palms up—in "a gesture of futility," Lichtenfels says. And *Persephone*'s folded wings droop and coil around her body, as if shielding the young goddess from her fate. (It was Lichtenfels's idea to represent *Persephone* as a winged creature.)

A graduate of the Philadelphia College of Art (Lichtenfels holds a BFA in illustration and filmmaking) and a former animator and model maker for Disney Studios in Burbank, California, the artist has developed an unparalleled technique for making dolls. She builds each piece from the inside out, first forming a skeleton out of heavy wire. To the skeleton she adds layers of batting to represent muscles and tendons. On top of this anatomically correct understructure Lichtenfels shapes and stitches nylon to create the figure's "skin."

Lichtenfels's dolls are astonishing in their realism; at the same time, they embody a powerful, haunting presence. Every inch of this silent figure speaks loudly of *Persephone*'s longing for life in the world of light. ✌

Persephone, front and side views,
24 inches, mixed-media
soft-sculpture, 1994

*The Bride and Her Ghost,
18 inches, polymer clay and
cloth, 1993*

The idea for *The Bride and Her Ghost* was born as Susanna Oroyan pondered what to do with two unfinished dolls. "I had a painted face and an unpainted one hanging on my bulletin board," she recalls. "I asked myself what that suggested. Answer: one living and one not." That macabre thought triggered her memory of *The Dybbuk*, a play written by Russian author Solomon Ansky in 1914. In Jewish folklore, a dybbuk is a restless spirit that seeks refuge in a living person's body. In Ansky's tale, a young man pines away for a woman betrothed to another. After his death, his spirit invades the body of the young bride. Oroyan interpreted the tale as a living, colorful bride haunted by a somber, ghostly twin. The dolls' faces are sculpted in polymer clay, covered with cloth, and painted; the bodies are cloth. The artist based the "living" bride's garment on traditional Russian folk bridal wear; the ghost's costume is a blend of antique laces. An accomplished author as well as an artist, Oroyan made her first doll in 1972. ❧

Christine Daaé, heroine of *The Phantom of the Opera*, is often depicted as a bride, although she does not wear wedding attire in Gaston Leroux's 1911 novel. As the suspenseful tale unfolds, the reader aches to know if the young opera singer will marry her beloved Raoul—the handsome Vicomte de Chagny—or join her mysterious mentor in his dark kingdom beneath the Paris Opera. This one-of-a-kind interpretation of Christine was created in 1990 by the Alexander Doll Company for auction at the annual Walt Disney World Doll and Teddy Bear Convention. Her late-nineteenth-century gown of sea-blue silk duchesse satin is embellished with pleated satin ribbon, Venise lace appliqués, and draped faux pearls. The underskirt is pleated brocade; the bustle is ivory and blue chiffon. *Christine*'s ensemble includes a veil of silver illusion, embroidered net gloves, a bouquet of ceramic and satin flowers, and crystal jewelry. In her hand she holds the phantom's mask. *Christine* has a vinyl head and arms, a hard-plastic body and legs, and sleep eyes.

Cinderella is every inch a princess in this pretty gown. A little girl's dream, the golden-haired beauty is crowned with a tiara of faux pearls. Her satiny bridal dress has a tulle overskirt and is embellished with satin roses, lace appliqués, and faux pearls. In her hand she carries a bouquet of white roses; on her feet she wears—but of course!—her "glass" slippers. The doll's head, limbs, and chest plate are porcelain; the torso is cloth. Designed by German artist Gaby Rademann for Ashton-Drake Galleries, *Cinderella Bride* debuted in 1998 and was the first edition in the Happily Ever After series of fairy tale brides. The artist, who's been sculpting dolls for more than twenty years, remembers the exact moment when the idea for Cinderella's wedding gown came to mind. "It was a romantic, warm summer evening," she says. "I was sitting among the lovely roses in my yard, and when the last drop of sunlight tickled my eyes, the golden shimmer created the vision of this wonderful dress." ❧

Cinderella Bride, 16½ inches, porcelain and cloth, 1998

*V*asilisa the Beautiful is a happily-ever-after Russian fairy tale about a courageous girl who wins the heart of a tsar. The youngster is tormented by a wicked stepmother and stepsisters; she also has to match wits with Baba Yaga, a witch with a taste for human flesh. But Vasilisa is aided by a magic doll, a gift from her loving mother. In 1993, Bavarian-born artist Brigitte Deval designed this lovely interpretation of Vasilisa as a bride for the Georgetown Collection. Based on traditional Russian wedding dress, *Vasilisa*'s ensemble includes a ruby-red tunic trimmed with gold braid, a white blouse with embroi-dered sleeves, and a green skirt with an embroidered apron. Her veil flows from a kokoshnik headpiece; in her hand is an embroidered handkerchief. *Vasilisa* has a porcelain head, porcelain legs and arms, and a cloth body, and was packaged with her "magic" doll and a story booklet. A pioneer of the art-doll genre, Deval admires Vasilisa not for her good looks, but for her unrelenting "determination and strength." ༖

Vasilisa the Beautiful, 20 inches,
porcelain and cloth, 1993

The first and only adult figure made by Mary Lee Sundstrom and Sandy Reinke, *Lorelei Lee* was inspired by the diamond-guzzling, man-hunting heroine of Anita Loos' 1925 novel *Gentlemen Prefer Blondes*. Introduced in an edition of 25 in 1996, *Lorelei Lee* was sold dressed as a flapper. One *Lorelei Lee*, however, was costumed by Reinke as a bride.

This Roaring Twenties wedding dress is a sassy, classy confection of vintage lace; vintage lace also trims the edge of the long net veil and the bouquet of handmade silk ribbon roses. Like all of Sundstrom and Reinke's dolls, she is carved from head to toe in wood; her hairdo is carved as well. To achieve this demure pose, Sundstrom carved *Lorelei Lee*'s arms and legs differently than the rest of the dolls in the edition. The 1920s bride was honored with a blue ribbon in the Modern, Costumed by Owner competition category at the 1997 conference of the United Federation of Doll Clubs. ∞

Lorelei Lee, 11 inches, wood, 1997

S he walks in beauty, like the night/Of cloudless climes and starry skies" wrote Lord Byron in 1815. For Wendy Lawton, the poet's passionate ode to "a heart whose love is innocent" was the perfect description of a bride. Dreamy and demure, Lawton's *She Walks in Beauty* doll pays homage to the poet's romantic words. She is garbed in a formal trained gown of tissue taffeta. Lace embroidered with iridescent glass beads decorates the bodice and the skirt's hem. Also lace, the leg-of-mutton sleeves have large tulle poufs. The bride's fingertip-length veil is attached to a headpiece of silk ribbons and dried flowers; dried and silk flowers make up her cascading bouquet. The fourth edition in the Lawton Doll Company's Timeless Ballads Collection, *She Walks in Beauty* is porcelain from head to toe. The doll was limited to an edition of 250. ❧

She Walks in Beauty, 18 inches, porcelain, 1988

Literature's most famous bride never reached the altar. She is, of course, the grim and melancholy Miss Havisham from Charles Dickens' *Great Expectations*. Jilted by her groom-to-be as she is dressing for her wedding, Miss Havisham lives the rest of her life wearing her bridal gown and just one shoe—exactly what she had on when she read the "dear John" note from her disloyal lover. When the novel's protagonist, Pip, meets Miss Havisham, he is startled by her attire, which he describes as made of "rich materials—satins, and lace, and silks." Young Pip is even more shocked, however, when he takes a closer look at Miss Havisham:

> *But, I saw that everything within my view which ought to be white, had been white long ago, and had lost its lustre, and was faded and yellow. I saw that the bride within the bridal dress had withered like the dress, and like the flowers, and had no brightness left but the brightness of her sunken eyes. I saw that the dress had been put upon the rounded figure of a young woman, and that the figure upon which it now hung loose, had shrunk to skin and bone.*

Miss Havisham has been interpreted in three-dimensional form by many dollmakers. Paul Crees and Peter Coe's version, made in 1992, shown on the opposite page, depicts the Dickens character as drawn, tired, and tearful (note the redness around her eyes and the loose fit of the gown at the bust), yet still proudly elegant. The doll wears a lace-trimmed gown of embroidered and beaded ivory silk with an overskirt of silk tulle. The doll's veil is also silk tulle. Limited to an edition of 25, *Miss Havisham* is made of poured wax.

Beloved dollmaker Robert McKinley, who passed away in 1994, was so enamored of this fictional character that he created five one-of-a-kind versions of her during his career. One of McKinley's fortes was sculpting elderly characters who were touched by sadness ("they just refuse to smile," he once said of his work), and this penchant for pathos is evident in his fourth and fifth *Miss Havisham* dolls. Created circa 1987, the fourth version, shown above left, is a frightening apparition in tattered finery. Her expression is forbidding; her pose, highly theatrical. Fellow artist Nancy Walters, a close friend of McKinley's, says that the last *Miss Havisham*, made circa 1989, and shown above right, "is the portrayal Bob said he always wanted to do: very angry." Both McKinley dolls are sculpted in polyform clay; the 1987 version has a cloth body with a wire armature. ❧

Miss Havisham, 28 inches, poured wax, 1992

Opposite page, far left: Miss Havisham, 22 inches, polyform clay and cloth, circa 1987

Opposite page, left: Miss Havisham, 12 inches, polyform clay, circa 1989

Moods, Musings, and Make-believe

For some dollmakers, the bride is a springboard to fantasy, the inspiration for a magical princess or forest fairy. For others, the bride is a symbol. As she makes the transition from single woman to married partner, she may represent bliss, hope, change, or maturity. *Happily Ever After*, an imaginative one-of-a-kind work by Nancy Wiley, reminds us to consider the many challenges posed by marriage. The large figure, costumed as a bride, "represents fate and marriage itself" says the artist. "The two smaller figures are being intertwined, or influenced, by the larger presence—marriage. Because when two people marry, they are forever part of something greater than themselves as individuals."

Created for debut in *Here Come the Bride Dolls*, *Happily Ever After* is one of Wiley's signature "pannier" dolls. In these figures, Wiley cleverly interprets the panniers of a dress—the pouffed sections at the upper skirt sides—as miniature stage curtains. The underskirt revealed by the parted "curtains" is transformed into a backdrop by the artist, who is also an accomplished painter. Dolls or marionettes, posed in front of the scene, play out a secret drama. (Wiley's pannier figures have made such a mark in the art doll field that actress Demi Moore, an enthusiastic collector, posed as a pannier puppeteer herself—with Wiley's help—for the June/July 1996 cover of *George* magazine.)

For *Happily Ever After*, Wiley painted a landscape and a castle perched high on a hill. "It symbolizes the 'happily ever after' destination of a fairy tale marriage," she explains. "However," the artist continues, "the journey is seldom a straight road, nor is it easy, symbolized in the winding path and river in the painting and the intertwined strings of the puppets."

The large doll has a sculpted Paperclay head, Paperclay arms and limbs, and a cloth body; her wig is raffia and her eyes are handpainted by the artist. Her gown is a blend of brocades embellished with Belgian lace, satin ribbons, and assorted trims; her tulle veil falls from a headpiece of lace and fabric flowers. The small bride and groom figures are porcelain, including their garments. (The bride's costume has several fabric components: the slip, veil, and bouquet.)

A graduate of the Rhode Island School of Design, Wiley began her own marital journey on October 13, 1991, when she wed Robert O'Brien. The couple lives in Hudson, New York. ಐ

Happily Ever After, 29 inches and 7½ inches, mixed media, 2000
Opposite page: Nancy Wiley and Robert O'Brien, October 13, 1991

A statuesque beauty, Isabelle Rose radiates confidence, strength, and poise. "She's not a silly, giggling bride. She's very sure about what she's doing," asserts her creator, Helen Kish.

Made of vinyl, the Isabelle Rose doll was introduced by Kish & Company in 1999. Part of the In an English Garden series, she represented a governess from the late nineteenth century. When invited to create a piece to debut in *Here Come the Bride Dolls*, Kish's thoughts immediately turned to this lovely lady. "I always expected that Isabelle Rose would have romance in her life," the artist says.

Isabelle Rose Wedding Day, a one-of-a-kind version of Isabelle Rose, is a collaboration between dollmaker Kish and clothing designer Rosemarie Ionker. (Well-versed in fashion design and history, the German-born Ionker earned a master's degree in dressmaking from the Institute of Fashion in Hamburg.) At first, Kish wanted Isabelle Rose to wear a Gibson Girl-inspired bridal ensemble. The doll's figure, however, posed a challenge: "Isabelle Rose is not a fashion doll, so she doesn't have a tiny waist. She's built more like a real woman, with a wider waistline, and we realized that the Gibson Girl style would not favor her," Kish explains.

Hence the doll is a marriage, of sorts, of styles: her upswept hairdo (it's made of mohair) and leg-of-mutton sleeves are typical of the Gibson Girl era, but the gown's low, rounded neckline and high waistline are reminiscent of the early-nineteenth-century Empire period.

Made of ivory silk, Isabelle Rose's gown has an overskirt and sleeves of dotted tulle. The overskirt is cut high in front, expanding to a long, dramatic train trimmed in re-embroidered lace. Also tulle, the veil flows from a glittering tiara of faux pearls and diamonds. Completing the bride's ensemble are a necklace of faux diamonds and pearls, matching earrings, and a bouquet of fabric flowers nestled in lace. ࿐

Isabelle Rose Wedding Day,
two views, 28 inches, vinyl,
2000

*H*éloïse is one of few artists who can create a doll that is pretty, charming, and childlike yet still has the dignified air of a work of art. This rare quality is readily seen in these dreamy damsels. *La Mariée* ("the bride"), shown at left, was made for "Vive La Mariée," an exhibit of antique and contemporary bride dolls held at the Musée de la Poupée et des Jouets Anciens in Nantes, France, in 1996. Crowned with a wreath of antique fabric flowers, *La Mariée* might reign in a fairy kingdom; or perhaps she is a nymph who makes her home in the woods. Posed atop a pedestal covered with antique red velvet, *La Mariée* wears a long-trained gown of silk accented with vintage lace on the bodice and sleeves. Vintage lace was also used for her veil. A one-of-a-kind work, the bride has a sculpted Fimo head, cloth body, and resin limbs.

Le Mariage de Marguerite, shown on the opposite page, was made in 2000 especially for debut in *Here Come the Bride Dolls*. With this piece, Héloïse wished to convey the radiant, almost beatific appearance of an eager young woman on her much longed-for wedding day. The piece is a one-of-a-kind version of Marguerite, a limited-edition doll also introduced in 2000. *Le Mariage de Marguerite* is garbed in some of the choicest fabrics from Héloïse's Nantes, France, studio. The high-necked, long-sleeved bodice is patterned silk tulle; the skirt is a blend of silk and vintage lace. Vintage lace also caps the sleeves. A train-length veil, also tulle, flows from a headpiece of vintage flowers and faux pearls.

Le Mariage de Marguerite has a resin head, resin arms and legs, and a cloth body. (Only this version of Marguerite has a body designed for standing; the others are seated.) Her expression and demeanor convey the artist's vision for the piece: that of a happy young bride "whose dream has come true."

La Mariée, 22 inches, Fimo,
resin, and cloth, 1996

Le Mariage de Marguerite,
22 inches, resin and cloth, 2000

Bridgette, 20 inches, porcelain and cloth, 1994

Described by her maker, Monika Mechling, as a "bride in waiting," *Bridgette* is a dreamy vision of romance. Her gown—the artist's interpretation of a Victorian wedding dress—has a draped silk chiffon bodice and a voluminous triple-layer skirt. The first layer, gathered in front, is georgette trimmed with lace; the second layer, also gathered, is embroidered lace from England. The topmost layer, made of silk chiffon, is open in front, revealing the two underskirts. The sleeves are silk chiffon capped with embroidered lace.

Bridgette's upswept hairdo is crowned with a wreath of silk roses; a trail of these flowers falls from her lap. The doll has a porcelain head, porcelain arms and legs, and a wired, cloth body; her expressive eyes are handpainted. Known to doll collectors by her first name only, Monika introduced *Bridgette* in 1994 in an edition of 35. (In 1993, the artist offered a one-of-a-kind version of the doll.) ʒ

Luci and Flower Girls,
28 inches and 19 inches, Fimo
and cloth, 1999

For Anna Avigail Brahms, a bride may represent "romance, longing, hope, or fear." *Luci* seems to be caught in a moment of contemplation. She holds her bouquet absent-mindedly as she meditates on her soon-to-be-married status. Her companions, two flower girls, likewise seem lost in dreams. Created in 1999, lovely *Luci* wears a shimmering gown of silk taffeta dotted at the hem and neckline with antique silk flowers. The gossamer veil is silk tulle. The flower girls are similarly garbed in taffeta and tulle. Each doll is one-of-a-kind and has a head sculpted of Fimo, sculpted Fimo arms and legs, and a wired cloth body. Long recognized as a pioneer of contemporary doll art (and an inspiration to many of her fellow artists), Brahms began sculpting and carving puppets and dolls in the 1970s. ❧

"When I think of a bride, I think of innocence, pleasure, all lovely things," Hildegard Günzel muses. Although best known for creating dolls of children, the German artist/designer has made several brides. In 1990, she created the *Bride Scene*, a vignette that depicts a bride *and* groom and four bridesmaids (the groom was not completed when the scene was photographed). "On the wedding day, everyone has to look their best!" she says of the well-dressed group. (All of the ladies are garbed in silk taffeta and antique laces.)

In 1992, Günzel made the *Fairy Bride*, another one-of-a-kind. Inspired by a ballet, this meditative beauty is no "ordinary" fairy; she is a queen. As befitting a royal, she wears an elaborate gown made of antique fabrics and lace. Her auburn ringlets are crowned with an elaborately beaded circlet of faux pearls and mingled with strands of faux pearls and fabric flowers.

Created in 2000, *Virginia* is the artist's smallest yet most spectacular bride to date. (She is just 18 inches; most of Günzel's dolls are at least 28 inches.) "I was obsessed with the idea of creating something very different from my limited editions, something delicate, and fragile," Günzel says. A former

fashion designer, she usually designs all her dolls' garments; however, this bride's ensemble was inspired by an antique gown. *Virginia*'s dress is silk satin covered with tulle. The bodice and skirt are beautifully embellished with antique lace; the bodice, which has lace sleeves, is also embroidered with faux pearls. Made of antique lace, the train-length veil is likewise embroidered with faux pearls. The headpiece is made of wax flowers, as is the bride's bouquet. Günzel made *Virginia* as a one-of-a-kind, but was so happy with the piece that she decided to offer a limited edition of twenty pieces instead.

Dolls have been a lifelong passion for this artist, who began sculpting in the 1970s. Through her Duisburg-based company, Porzellanpuppenmanufaktur Hildegard Günzel, she offers limited-edition dolls; she also creates a one-of-a-kind work every year. Most of her pieces—and all of the brides shown here—have wax-covered, porcelain heads, arms, and legs; cloth bodies; and blown glass eyes.

With her bride dolls, Günzel challenges the viewer to make up his or her own story. "I want everyone to interpret for themselves what each doll means," she says. ဢ

Virginia, 18 inches, wax over porcelain and cloth, 2000
Opposite page far left: Fairy Bride, 43 inches, wax over porcelain and cloth, 1992
Opposite page left: Bride Scene, 35 inches (bride) and 29 inches (attendants), wax-over-porcelain and cloth, 1990

list of Bob Mackie's credits and kudos would run longer than a cathedral-length bridal veil. The California-born designer has created fashions and home furnishings, scarves and stationery. He's designed costumes for television, film, and Broadway, earning eight Emmy awards, thirty-one Emmy nominations, and three Oscar nominations in the process. But Mackie's most famous and widely loved creations are the glamorous, glittering garments that he's made for trend-setting superstars like Cher, Diana Ross, and, of course, Barbie.

The celebrated couturier created his first design for Barbie in 1990. Fifth in the Mackie series, *Empress Bride Barbie* was released in 1992. A commanding presence indeed, she wears a gown that's fit for a queen. The bodice and overskirt are made of ivory brocade decorated with iridescent sequins, beads, and golden embroidery. The wide, layered underskirt is pleated tulle. A tulle veil cascades from a crownlike headpiece adorned with sequins, beads, and marquis-cut rhinestones. A beaded choker, faux pearl drop earrings, and a bouquet of white and gold roses complete this majestic ensemble.

"It's the only bride doll I've ever done," Mackie says. "I wanted something that represented every girl's fantasy about the wedding gown, something a girl would want to wear if she really were a princess and was getting married. That was the whole idea."

Years before Mackie created this dazzling design for Barbie, he created hundreds of wedding gowns for real-life brides and brides on film. "When I was very young, I worked for Edith Head at Paramount. She always had me work on all the bridal gowns, because I had a good feeling for it. I could do fifty in a day—big sketches in color," he says. Mackie has also designed bridal wear for celebrities such as Cher ("it didn't look like a bridal gown; it had a corselet top!") and Linda Carter ("her gown was very, very romantic"). In 2000, he announced plans to launch a new line of ready-to-wear bridal fashions.

Empress Bride Barbie is one of the most coveted Barbie dolls ever made for collectors. The doll originally sold for about $200, but a mint-in-box example commanded as much as $1,300 on the secondary market in 2000, according to fashion doll expert and author A. Glenn Mandeville. Evidently, with a Mackie design, all that glitters *is* golden. &

Empress Bride Barbie,
11½ inches, vinyl, 1992

For her creator, Wendy Lawton, *The Blushing Bride* represents "the emotion of the wedding day." The artist says, "What I tried to capture was the unique blend of fear and anticipation, the mixed feelings of nostalgia and hope for the future, and the state of being poised between childhood and womanhood." A one-of-a-kind piece created by The Lawton Doll Company and auctioned at the 1998 Walt Disney World Teddy Bear and Doll Convention, *The Blushing Bride* wears a silk organza gown. Pearl and silk ribbon embroidery decorates the front of the dress, from the shoulders to the top of the wide ruffle at the skirt's hem. The edges of the billowy, tulle veil are rolled and trimmed with pearls. *The Blushing Bride* has a porcelain head, upper torso, and arms; the lower torso and legs are wood. ❧

The Blushing Bride, 18 inches,
porcelain and wood, 1998

$\mathcal{T}$eresa, a moody beauty, is one in a series of fairy brides having second thoughts about their upcoming nuptials. Will she, or won't she? You decide! Created by Marilyn Stivers in 1997, the one-of-a-kind bride is swathed in handmade vintage lace. Her short-sleeved, cropped bodice and long, flowing skirt are embellished with tiny pale-pink and light-blue crystal beads and faux pearls. Her voluminous auburn hairdo is adorned with a vintage silver metallic bow and one velvet violet. The artist, who enjoys recreating the female form, sculpted *Teresa* from head to toe in synthetic clay. "My goal in making a doll is to make a little piece of beauty," she says. ❧

Teresa, 12 inches, clay, 1997

Light, airy, and carefree, the whimsical bride shown on the opposite page looks as if she's about to float away on a dream. "As I worked on her, I constantly kept the idea of lightness—the image of a feather—in mind," says her creator, Nita Angeletti. Like a fairy godmother, the New York City-based artist turns materials into magic. For *Bride With Parasol,* made for debut in *Here Come the Bride Dolls,* she turned antique ecru and white laces into a short, frothy dress (it's inspired by a ballerina's tutu) and a cloud-like parasol. Silk rosebuds and lace became a cascading headpiece. A fine golden mesh, entwined around the figure's arms, adds texture; a strand of tiny pearls, tied in a bow behind the bride's neck and hanging down her back, adds glamour. Fine tulle makes perfect "stockings," and tinkling antique brass bells from India add a decorative edging to the lace parasol.

A graduate of The Juilliard School and a former professional dancer and actress, the artist began making dolls in 1986. Her dance background is evident in her work (most of her pieces either depict dancers or incorporate a feeling of movement), as is her passion for fashion and decorative art.

Bride With Parasol is a one-of-a-kind version of a cast-resin figure made from Angeletti's original sculpture. Typical of the artist's flamboyant style, the doll is richly painted, layer by layer, with a multicolored palette. To add even more texture, Angeletti wrapped the figure's legs with fine wire. *Bride*

With Parasol is fixed to a mirrored metal base and would look right at home on a bride's vanity table.

Another delightful accessory for the bride's dresser is the wee wedding fairy shown above. Perhaps the smallest bride in the world, she resides in a handmade beaded trinket box. Created by Scottish-born artist Mirren Barrie, who excels at both dollmaking and embroidery, the 2¼-inch bride is an ingenious mix of materials. Her head is a bead covered with embroidery thread; her poseable body is a blend of paper, wire, and beads; her wings are nylon ribbon. Layers of gold- and silver-flecked Japanese paper make up the doll's ankle-length wedding dress; her fan-shaped veil is made of the same paper. The fairy bride carries a bouquet of daisies; one daisy adorns her golden hair.

Made of white felt, the trinket box is as lovely as the bride. Barrie embellished the box's lid with a pearl-tissue flower with wired petals and embroidered leaves; a cluster of floss-covered bead "berries" in white, cream, and ecru; and a crystal-bead dragonfly with gold-dusted paper wings. The fanciful *Fairy Bride in Box* was created to debut in *Here Come the Bride Dolls* and is a limited edition of five. ಐ

Above: Fairy Bride in Box, 2¼ inches, mixed media, 2000
Opposite page: Bride With Parasol, 21 inches, mixed media, 2000

escribed by her maker, Helen Kish, as "the bride of every sailor who has given his last breath for her love," the *Bride of the Sea* is at once majestic and melancholy. Her diaphanous gown is as frothy as a wave; the curly locks of her pale-blonde mohair wig suggest the sinuous tendrils of underwater plants. The bride wears a low-necked, slightly off-the-shoulder body suit of pale-peach stretch mesh. The bodice is finished with appliqués, faux pearls, and crystal beads; the sleeves, which end in points, are encrusted with faux pearls and beads. The skirt is tulle, gathered at waist. No veil for this briny bride: Her headpiece is a tulle cap embellished with beads, faux pearls, and silk ribbon embroidery. The long-limbed figure is made of porcelain; her eyes are handpainted by the artist. *Bride of the Sea* was introduced in 1997 in an edition of ten. &

*Bride of the Sea, 27 inches,
porcelain, 1997*

You can bet they did the Bunny Hop at this bride and groom's wedding reception! Commissioned by a couple who wanted to present their daughter with a unique wedding gift, the *Bridal Couple* was created by Akira Blount in 1995. The dolls wear quaint, old-fashioned garments made out of antique cottons and laces. Her shoes are fabric; his are leather. The bride and groom are made of cloth from ears to toes. The cloth bunny heads, which are stiffened with layers of gesso, are actually removable masks. Underneath the masks are human heads of cloth, with needle-modeled and handpainted facial features. A one-of-a-kind work, the *Bridal Couple* is the only wedding-themed piece ever created by Blount, who is as well-known among collectors of fine arts and crafts as she is among doll enthusiasts. ཚ

Bridal Couple, 18 inches, cloth, 1995

Global Visions

Festive, elaborate, and often vibrantly colored, bridal attire from around the world reflects the many diverse and often ancient traditions associated with marriage. Bright red, considered a symbol of fertility, is worn by Hindu, Islamic, and Chinese brides. While American brides often limit their jewelry to a strand of pearls and matching earrings, an Indian bride may be laden with gold jewelry and coins, representing her dowry. Many African brides adorn themselves with elaborate beaded jewelry and body ornaments; a silver pendant shaped like a hand is believed to ward off the evil eye for the Berber bride of North Africa. A Japanese bride wears a white fabric hood or headdress, called the *tsuno-kakushi*, which conceals the woman's "horns of jealousy."

Many women around the world transform their bodies into works of art for their wedding. A Masai bride of East Africa paints her skin and hair with red ocher. Brides from India, the Middle East, and parts of North Africa decorate the palms of their hands and feet (and sometimes the forearms and lower legs) with henna.

The latter tradition inspired Wendy Lawton to create Gita, who represents a Hindu bride-to-be from India. "The day before her wedding, Gita and the women of her family gather for the mehndi ritual," the dollmaker says. During this ceremony, intricate henna designs are applied to the bride's palms and feet by either a relative, friend or mehndi artist. "Gita's future mother-in-law will apply at least one stroke as a sign of her blessing on the union," Lawton says.

Working from pictures of real-life Hindu brides, Lawton painted a modified version of an Indian design onto the bride-to-be's palms and forearms. Made in 2000 exclusively for debut in *Here Come the Bride Dolls*, Gita wears a sari made from a hand-batiked silk scarf. Her bodice, or *choli*, is silk. Titled *Mehndi Ritual*, the one-of-a-kind doll has a porcelain head and upper body, porcelain arms, wooden legs, and a wooden lower body. ❧

An Indian bride's hands, painted with henna

*Mehndi Ritual, 14 inches,
porcelain and wood, 2000*

Mindiyana, 40 inches,
porcelain and cloth, 1996
Opposite page: Nkike, 40 inches,
porcelain and cloth, 1996

raveling in East Africa in the 1990s, Philip Heath was struck by the beauty of a young Masai girl named Nkike, who was taking part in a ceremony celebrating her betrothal. "All the girls were painted with red ocher," Heath told the author in a 1996 interview. "They mix the ocher with animal fat, and rub it onto their bodies. They dip the leather skins they wear as skirts also into the red ocher, so everything was glistening and slightly oily. . . . There was dust and noise and singing, and goats and cattle moving in the background. The dust was sticking to [the girls'] bodies, and they were jumping and singing."

Once back in his studio, Heath modeled the doll *Nkike*, shown on the opposite page, from his vivid memories as well as from photographs. Soulful and solemn, the doll offers a revealing, if fleeting, glimpse of a faraway culture. *Nkike*'s chest is adorned with an intricate pattern of raised scars, a form of tattooing that is traditional among the Masai. Her earlobes are stretched from the weight of her heavy jewelry. Her garment is made of black goat skin, and she wears necklaces and a headpiece of red glass beads. The young bride holds a gourd that's painted red on the inside, representing the ceremonial ocher. An antique, the gourd was purchased by Heath in Africa, as was the Masai stool on which *Nkike* sits.

Heath traveled extensively during the 1990s, photographing and observing children around the world to serve as models for his porcelain dolls, as well as for a line of vinyl dolls produced by the German firm Götz. While abroad, Heath observed everyday life and community celebrations. In Rajasthan, India, he attended a wedding, the inspiration for *Mindiyana*, shown at left, a young bride getting dressed for her special day. Dressed in red, the color for Indian brides, she wears billowy trousers (*sahvar*) banded at the ankle, a skirt, and a cropped jacket made of satin and silk. Heath painted the bride's long scarf (*ohrna*) in gold, using an Indian motif. (The scarf itself is antique Indian fabric.) He also painted her feet and hands, simulating the traditional henna decorations used for brides. *Mindiyana*'s hair ornament and nose jewelry are also from India.

Both made in 1996, *Nkike* and *Mindiyana* have porcelain heads and upper bodies, porcelain arms and legs, cloth lower bodies with metal armatures, and blown-glass eyes. Each doll was limited to an edition of two. Proficient in many facets of art (he studied drawing, painting, and sculpture and later served as head of the ceramics department at Malvern College in England), the British-born Heath began making dolls in 1985. ✤

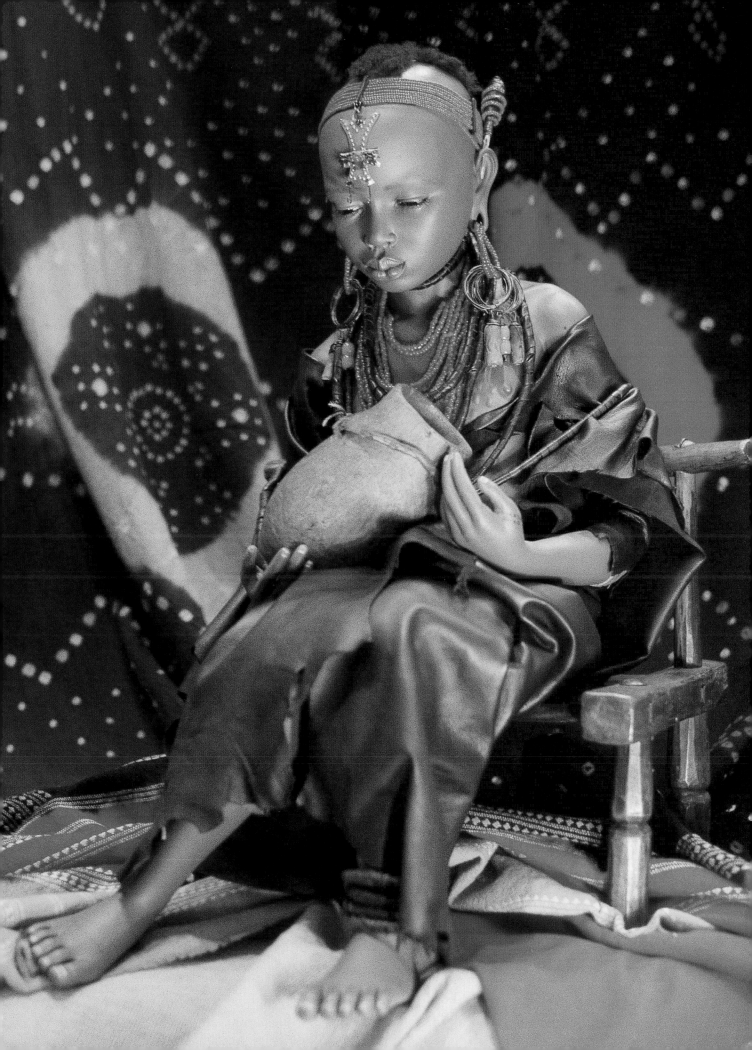

The Songhai of Mali (in West Africa) are known for their elaborate coiffures. Denita Nyree Piltzer's *Songhai Bride* wears an eye-catching hairstyle called *Homborienne*. The hair is intricately plaited and adorned with charms, beads, and gold- and silver-colored coins. "Heirloom ornaments like these are passed down from a mother to her daughter at the time of marriage," the artist says. (A Songhai bride also weaves protective talismans into her hairdo.) Piltzer enjoys incorporating African traditions into her dolls, which are made of resin and have handpainted eyes. Part of the Tribal Art Happy Doll series, the *Songhai Bride* wears a loose-fitting gown of patterned rayon. The costume is Piltzer's interpretation of a garment worn by a Mali bride photographed by Angela Fisher and Carol Beckwith, whose work appears in books and calendars. ✣

Songhai Bride, 15 inches, resin, 1995

"The young girl Mavra is getting married today. She is wearing the best of all dresses—the wedding costume," reads the tag that accompanies this magnificently costumed doll, which was made by the Moscow-based Alexandra Company in 1991. The bride's ensemble is a reproduction of an early-nineteenth-century wedding costume worn by a peasant from the town of Galich in Russia's Kostroma province. *Mavra* wears a jacket and skirt of deep-red rayon, richly embellished with filigree buttons, gold laces, and embroidery. She also wears an embroidered and beaded white muslin blouse and a white underskirt. Her *kokoshnik* (headdress) is embroidered with gold and silver thread and faux pearls. *Mavra*'s white muslin kerchief, also embroidered in gold, is a gift from her husband-to-be, as are her lace-trimmed boots. The Alexandra Company was founded in 1989 by designer Alexandra Koukinova, who is inspired by Russian history, fairy tales, and folk costumes. *Mavra* is made of cotton cloth and has embroidered and painted facial features. ๑

Mavra, 30 inches, cloth, 1991

Herero woman in ekori *headdress, 1953*
Opposite page: Herero, 10 inches, polyform clay, 2000

Created by husband-and-wife team Jodi and Richard Creager, *Herero* is a serene portrayal of a newly married young woman. While reading about the Herero, a people of Southern Africa, the artists came aross a striking photograph taken in 1953 by anthropologist Gordon D. Gibson. The photo, shown at left, is of an elderly Herero woman, lost in thought. The Creagers were intrigued by her appearance as well as by her elaborate headpiece, which, they learned, is called an *ekori*.

"The *ekori* was worn on special occasions by married Herero women and was worn by brides," Jodi Creager says. Made of leather and decorated all around with rows of iron beads, the *ekori* is crowned with three triangular points, or horns. A "veil" made of softened animal skin, which can be rolled up or lowered to hide the face, is attached to the front. "When a new bride was brought to her husband's home, she rolled down the veil, covering her face," Richard Creager says.

Greatly moved by the Herero's tragic history (at the beginning of the twentieth century, the Herero population was decimated after an unsuccessful rebellion against the German government in Africa), the Creagers created *Herero* as a tribute. A scaled-down version of an *ekori*, the doll's leather headdress has a hand-punched design and is adorned with sterling-silver beads, which simulate the iron beads on a real *ekori*. The woman wears a leather-and-cotton garment and a necklace of beads and leather.

The *ekori* is no longer worn by the Herero; in 1953, when the photo that inspired this doll was taken, the headdress was worn by only a few "old-fashioned" women, Gordon Gibson says. (Married Herero women, who should not be seen in public with bare heads, now wear cotton headdresses.) A former curator of African Anthropology at the Smithsonian Institution, Gibson explains that the horns on the *ekori* "symbolize the Herero's close relationship to their herds of cattle," which traditionally provided much of their food and clothing. That the *ekori* has three horns instead of two represents the Herero's superiority to the cattle, he adds.

A former portrait painter, Jodi Creager sculpted the doll's head and hands in polyform clay; she also painted the face. Richard Creager sculpted the body, arms, legs, and feet. To the artists, who began making dolls in the 1980s, *Herero* represents "sheer simplicity and beauty." ❧

Rie and Hideki Ishii,
April 15, 2000
Opposite page: Little Bride, 6 inches,
washi paper and cotton, 1996

ittle Bride, created by Kyoko Nakanishi in 1996, celebrates the beauty and solemnity of a traditional Japanese wedding. Just six inches high, the doll wears a scaled-to-size version of an ensemble that a Japanese bride might wear today, as shown by real-life bride Rie Ishii, the daughter of one of the artist's friends. *Little Bride* is garbed in a *uchikake*, or bridal robe, of white, worn with a white under-kimono tied at the waist with the familiar *obi* sash. Tucked into her *obi* are a *kaiken*, or dagger, in white; and a *kaishi*, a small square of washi paper, in pink. "People believe that the sword—even a small dagger—protects the wearer from evil. For the bride, it is like an amulet or charm," Nakanishi explains. The *kaishi*, which is usually enclosed in a holder, is versatile. "You can use it as a handkerchief or even a small plate for cookies!" the artist says.

Little Bride holds a fan, or *snesu*, a symbol of her wide, open future. Her elaborate hairstyle is called the *shimada katsura*, and is worn only by brides. Her white headpiece—the *tsuno-kakushi*—shields the groom from her "horns of jealousy." (The real-life *tsuno-kakushi* covers the bride's head.) After the ceremony, this headpiece is removed. (The Japanese bridegroom wears a traditional outfit as well, as demonstrated by Hideki Ishii. His attire includes a white under-kimono; a short black kimono coat, or *haori*; wide pleated pants, or *hakama*; split-toed socks, *tabi*; and thong sandals, *zori*.)

Like all of Nakanishi's dolls, *Little Bride* is made primarily of washi paper. Handcrafted by skilled artisans from fiber taken from the inner bark of the mulberry tree, washi has been made in Japan for over one thousand years. The doll's head, body, and limbs are a blend of washi paper, cotton, and wire. Her costume and hair are made entirely of washi, embellished with beads and other small trim. As is traditional for washi dolls, the face is unpainted.

Nakanishi began making washi dolls in the 1960s, reviving an art form that dates to the thirteenth century. In 1965, the artist and her husband established the Yamato Ohtori Washi Doll studio, through which she has taught the washi tradition to hundreds of students. Elaborate dioramas created by the studio are displayed in more than sixty locations in Japan, including airports, museums, and public buildings; they have also been exhibited in the United States, France, Canada, and other nations. Each diorama may include up to 2,500 dolls. ✍

Radiant in her jewel-bright silk and velvet garments, this Turkish bride is off to the home of her husband-to-be. She is crying and will use her dainty embroidered handkerchief to dry her tears. "She is sad to leave her family, but happy that she is getting married," says her creator, Lütfiye Batukan. "In Turkish there is an expression, 'I cry and go at the same time.' It is used to express contradictory feelings."

Fatma the Bride wears a traditional wedding costume from West Anatolia. The style dates back to the mid-eighteenth century and, according to Batukan, is still worn by some brides in the region ("but not in the cities," she says). The ensemble includes a three-piece dress (*uc etek*), a blouse (*gomlek*), wide pants (*shalvar*), a short jacket (*cepken*), and three belts (one is tied around the bride's waist by her father when she leaves home). On her head, the bride wears a pale-purple embroidered scarf made of vintage fabric, an embroidered headdress, and a red veil that will cover her face. "Red is the color of happiness, and a red scarf is usually worn by brides," Batukan says. "In some regions," she adds, "a bride wears all the colors of the rainbow on her head." The spangles on the headdress represent golden coins—the bride's dowry—as does her beaded and spangled necklace.

It was traditional for the bride to ride to her bridegroom's house on horseback, the artist says. Her parents would walk alongside, carrying the bride's belongings and trousseau. (If the groom lived far away, horses and donkeys were used to transport the bride's possessions.) "This convoy was called the 'Bride's Troops,'" Batukan says. Fatma's horse, also made by the artist, is handsomely decorated for the day with brocade fabric, beads, and other trimmings.

Like all of Batukan's figures, *Fatma the Bride* is a blend of cotton, tragacanth (a plant-derived gum), paper, and wire, and is handpainted by the artist. Made in 2001, the piece is a one-of-a-kind. (Also one-of-a-kind, the figures representing the Bride's Troops were made in the 1990s.)

Batukan has been making dolls since the 1960s and has exhibited her work in Egypt, Poland, Germany, and other nations. Dressed in authentic folk costumes, her pieces pay homage to Turkish culture. "My main goal is to preserve Turkish traditions and history," she says. ❧

Above: Fatma the Bride and Bride Troops, 16 inches, mixed-media, 1990s

Fatma the Bride,
16 inches, mixed-media, 2001

Epilogue: The Bride's Journey

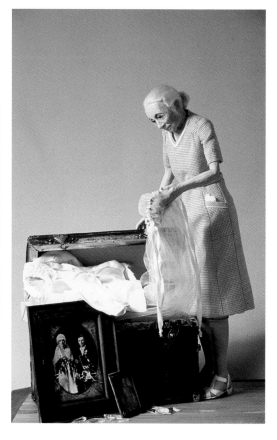

These evocative vignettes, by three different artists, remind us that the wedding day is only one stop on a journey of a lifetime. Made in 1999, *Gail and Neil—25th Wedding Anniversary* depicts a happily-ever-after couple reminiscing about their life together. Carved in wood by Michael Langton, the one-of-a-kind duo was commissioned as an anniversary gift. The artist videotaped the real Gail and Neil interacting and referred to the tapes as he carved their portraits. The dolls' outfits are copies (made by Pam Hamel) of Gail and Neil's real clothing, and each accessory in the scene has meaning. Neil is a dentist, so beside him are miniaturized dental journals; Gail does needlework, so Langton's partner, Jan Wilensky, stitched a wee anniversary sampler. The album that Gail holds contains reduced versions of actual photos from the couple's twenty-five years together, from their wedding pictures to pictures of their children's graduations.

An untitled work by Robert McKinley, the elderly woman shown above right is contemplating her wedding day mementos. She has unpacked her old photographs, including the wedding portrait, and holds her veil as if it were a precious jewel. There's longing in her face, to be sure, but there's a gentle glow of happiness, too. Beautifully sculpted in polyform clay, the face of this former bride tells us all we need to know about wedding day bliss. Created circa 1987, the work is a one-of-a-kind.

Grandma's Wedding Dress, 1930's, an edition of two, was created by Maria Åhrén in 1998. The lovely doll (a blend of porcelain, polyform clay, and cloth), shown on the opposite page, brings the bride's journey full circle. A young woman of the 1930s, she has carefully unpacked her grandmother's 1890s wedding gown so she could try it on. Her dreamy expression tells us that she is imagining her own wedding day. Perhaps she has already met the man of her dreams; perhaps not. But as she prepares to crown her head with her grandmother's vintage veil, she symbolizes the hopes and dreams of all brides, past, present, and future. ❧

Bibliography

The following sources were consulted during the preparation of this text.

Books

Bullard, Helen. *Dorothy Heizer: The Artist and Her Dolls*. New York: National Institute of American Doll Artists, 1972.

————————. *The American Doll Artist*. Vol. 1. Falls Church, Va.: The Summit Press Ltd., 1977.

Callister, J. Herbert, ed. *Dress from Three Centuries: Wadsworth Atheneum*. Hartford, Conn.: Wadsworth Atheneum, 1976.

Cook, Carolyn. *Gene*. Grantsville, Md: Hobby House Press, Inc., 1998.

Cross, Wilbur, and Ann Novotny. *White House Weddings*. New York: David McKay Co., Inc., 1967.

Davis, William Stearns. *A Day in Old Rome*. New York: Biblo and Tannen, 1928.

Dickens, Charles. *Great Expectations*. New York: Dodd, Mead, & Company, Inc., 1942.

Field, Rachel. *Hitty: Her First Hundred Years*. New York: The Macmillan Company, 1929.

Finnegan, Stephanie. *Madame Alexander Dolls: An American Legend*. New York: Alexander Doll Company, Inc. and Portfolio Press Corporation, 1999.

Fisher, Angela. *Africa Adorned*. New York: Harry N. Abrams, Inc., Publishers, 1984.

Gibson, Charles D. *The Gibson Girl and Her America: The Best Drawings of Charles Dana Gibson*. Edmund Gillon, ed. Mineola, New York: Dover Publications, Inc., 1969.

Jackson, Ellen. *Here Come the Brides*. New York: Walker and Company, 1998.

Jerde, Judith. *Encyclopedia of Textiles*. New York: Facts On File, Inc., 1992.

Johnston, Estelle, ed. *To Have and To Hold*. Souvenir book from the 48th Annual Convention of the United Federation of Doll Clubs, July 27- August 1, Anaheim, California.

Jones, Leslie. *Happy Is the Bride the Sun Shines On: Wedding Beliefs, Customs, and Traditions*. Chicago: Contemporary Books, 1995.

Kalmar, Bobbie. *18th Century Clothing*. New York: Crabtree Publishing Company, 1993.

Kelley, Kitty. *Elizabeth Taylor, The Last Star*. New York: Simon & Schuster, 1981.

Kennett, Frances. *Ethnic Dress*. Great Britain: Reed International Books Limited, 1995. Reprinted in the United States by Facts On File, Inc.

Lewis, Mary E., and Dorothy Dignam. *The Marriage of Diamonds and Dolls*. New York: H.L. Lindquist Publications, 1947.

McBride-Mellinger, Maria. *The Perfect Wedding*. San Francisco: Collins Publishers, 1997.

Morton, Andrew. *Diana, Her True Story—In Her Own Words*. New York: Simon & Schuster, 1997.

Murphy, Brian. *The World of Weddings: An Illustrated Celebration*. New York: Paddington Press, 1978.

Odenrider, Ada Bridgman. *Wedding Belles of Dolls and Costumes*. Seattle, Wash.: Ada Bridgman Odenrider, 1969.

Olian, JoAnne, ed. *Wedding Fashions 1862-1912: 380 Costume Designs from "La Mode Illustrée."* Mineola, New York: Dover Publicatons, Inc., 1994.

Peacock, John. *20th Century Fashion*. London: Thames & Hudson, Ltd., 1993.

Roman, Inc. *Classic Brides of the Century*. Roselle, Ill.: Roman, Inc., 1988.

Smith, Marie, and Louise Durbin. *White House Brides*. Washington, D.C.: Acropolis Books, 1966.

Spada, James. *Grace: The Secret Lives of a Princess*. Garden City, N.Y.: Doubleday & Company, Inc., 1987.

Tierney, Tom. *Bride and Groom Fashion Paper Dolls*. Mineola, N.Y.: Dover Publications, Inc., 1990.

Tober, Barbara. *The Bride. A Celebration*. New York: Harry N. Abrams, 1984.

Articles

Bischoff, Karen. "A Childhood Love Turns Into a Lifelong Passion." *Dolls,* Vol. 10, October 1991, pp.73-77.

Fecher, Louise. "The Babies and Beauties of Helen Kish." *Dolls,* Vol. 7, March/April 1988, pp. 36-39.
_____. "The Artist As Philosopher." *Dolls,* Vol. 8, November 1989, pp. 58-62.
_____. "A Sense of Style." *Dolls,* Vol. 13, June/July 1994, pp. 51-55.
_____. "Global Warming." *Dolls,* Vol. 15, August 1996, pp. 91-94.
_____. "A Niche of Their Own." *Dolls,* Vol. 17, January 1997, pp. 62-65.

Goddu, Krystyna Poray. "The Pull of Memories." *Dolls,* Vol. 6, September/October 1987, pp. 44-47.
_____. "Margaret Woodbury Strong's Incredible Doll Collection." *Dolls,* Vol. 1, Winter 1982 (premiere issue), pp. 32-37.

John F. Kennedy Library. "The Wedding of Jacqueline Lee Bouvier and John Fitzgerald Kennedy." Retrieved September 20, 2000, from the World Wide Web: http://www.jfklibrary.org/jbkwed.htm.

Noble, John. "Here Come the Brides." *Dolls,* Vol. 13, January 1994, pp. 62-65.

Rondon, Nayda. "Lütfiye Batukan: Turkish Delight." *Dolls,* Vol. 19, September 2000, pp. 53-54.

TheRussianHouse.com. "Vasilisa the Beautiful." ©1997. Retrieved November 8, 2000, from the World Wide Web: http://www.therussianhouse.com/vasilla.htm.

WeddingChannel.com. "The Evolution of Wedding Fashion." ©1997-2000. Retrieved December 19, 2000, from the World Wide Web: http:www.weddingchannel.com

Whitton, Margaret. "A Doll For Elizabeth's Jubilee." *New York-Pennsylvania Collector*. July 1977, p. 4-B.

Acknowledgments

The author would like to thank all the artists and companies who shared photographs and information for publication in this book, with special thanks to Nita Angeletti, Mirren Barrie, Charles Batte, Stephanie Blythe, Joanne Callander, Edna Dali, Héloïse, Dorothy Hoskins, Helen Kish, Wendy Lawton, Heather Maciak, Robert Tonner, Annie Wahl, Nancy Wiley, Zofia and Henry Zawieruszynki, and the Alexander Doll Company, who honored this project by creating exclusive dolls for debut in its pages, as well as Mel Odom, Beth Maxwell, and the Gene Team, who offered photos of rare prototype Gene dolls. The author would also like to thank family, friends, and associates for generously (and bravely) sharing their wedding photos, especially Mrs. Raffaela Palmiere, who was willing to trust a stranger with her wedding portrait. The author would also like to acknowledge Gordon D. Gibson, Estelle Johnston, A. Glenn Mandeville, John Darcy Noble, Lia Sargent, Barbara Steiker, Carol Stover, and Phyllis West, who shared information, photos, and insights; Leah Maxwell and Patricia Hogan of the Strong Museum, Jennifer Brathovde of the Library of Congress, Antoinette Ranioloi and the staff of the Crestwood branch of the Yonkers Public Library, Charles Batte, and NIADA-Archive-keepers Maralyn Christoffersen and Betty Hodges, for their research assistance; Lynn Amos, for lending her artistic eye; and, lastly, my editor, Krystyna Poray Goddu, for her patience and her support of this project.

Directory and Index

*designed doll or costume for manufacturer
**address withheld on request
+ deceased

Manufacturers

Alexander Doll Company, Inc. 7, 18, 19,
        36, 37, 54, 68, 73, 80, 101, 115
615 West 131st St.
New York, NY 10027
212-283-5900
www.madamealexander.com

Alexandra Company/Russian Dolls 145
P.O. Box 9
Lynbrook, NY 11563
646-391-0151
russian_dolls@hotmail.com

The Ashton-Drake Galleries 38, 39, 40,
        42, 44, 45, 48, 87, 93, 116, 117
9200 N. Maryland Ave.
Niles, IL 60714-1397
800-346-2460 (Ashton-Drake and
Georgetown dolls)
888-FOR-GENE (Gene dolls)

Corolle 58, 59
268 Wilton Rd.
Westport, CT 06880
203-222-1005
www.corolledolls.com

Daddy's Long Legs/KVK, Inc 41, 74,
300 Bank St.
Southlake, TX 76092
817-481-4800
www.daddystrunk.com

The Franklin Mint.........................29, 99, 105
Franklin Center, PA 19091
800-THE-MINT
www.franklinmint.com

Kish & Company 91, 124, 138
8250 West Coal Mine Ave., #10
Littleton, CO 80123
303-972-0053
kishco@msn.com

The Lawton Doll Company ..20, 119, 134, 141
548 N. First St.
Turlock, CA 95380
209-632-3655
wlawton@mindspring.com

Mattel, Inc./Barbie Collectibles 7, 52, 62,
        63, 81, 104, 106, 107, 132
333 Continental Blvd.
El Segundo, CA 90245
800-524-8694
www.barbiecollectibles.com

Lee Middleton Original Dolls 109
480 Olde Worthington Rd.
Westerville, OH 43082
614-901-0604
www.leemiddleton.com

Porzellanpuppenmanufaktur Hildegard
Günzel...130, 131
Dr-Alfred-Herrhausen-Allee 60
D-47228 Duisburg, Germany
49-2065-66199
designby@hildegardguenzel.com
www.hildegardguenzel.com

Robert Tonner Doll Company......47, 50, 51,
        60, 61, 77, 89
459 Hurley Ave.
Hurley, NY 12443
845-339-9537
www.roberttonner.com

United States Historical Society.................25
First and Main Sts.
Richmond, VA 23219
804-648-4736

The Vogue Doll Company....................75, 88
P.O. Box 756
Oakdale, CA 95361
209-848-0300
www.voguedolls.com

The Susan Wakeen Doll Company 55
425 Bantam Rd.
P.O. Box 1321
Litchfield, CT 06759
860-567-0007

*designed doll or costume for manufacturer
**address withheld on request
+ deceased

Picture Credits

pages 6, 42, right: Courtesy of Bernice Fecher; page 7, top right and bottom: Walter Pfeiffer; pages 7, top left, 10, 13, 108: Courtesy of Strong Museum, Rochester, New York. ©2000; page 8, left: Photo: Lynton Gardiner. Museum of the City of New York, Gift of Mrs. Edward C. Moen. 46.146.47. page 8, right: Photo: Helga Photo Studio. Museum of the City of New York. Gift of Raffaela Celentano Palmiere. 98.105.1; page 9: Emil Saracino/Courtesy of Raffaela Celentano Palmiere; page 11: Library of Congress NYWT&S-BIOG-ENGLAND, ROYAL FAMILY; page 12, 120, 152, right: Courtesy of the NIADA Archive (National Institute of American Doll Artists); page 14, top: Russell Studio/Courtesy of Anna Petro; pages 14, bottom, 25, full page: George Petro; page 15, left: Courtesy of Gigi Williams; pages 16, 17: Peter Marcus Photography; pages 18, 19, 36, 37, top left and right, 54, 69, 73, 80, 101, 115: ©Alexander Doll Company Inc./Provided courtesy of The Alexander Doll Company, Inc.; pages 24, 32, 33, 35, 67, top, 70, 71, 136, 137, 152, left: Jerry Anthony; page 26: DOWIC Fotografi/Courtesy of Statens Museum for Kunst, Copenhagen, *The Bride Room* by Henrik Olrik, 1859; page 28: Reprinted from *Wedding Fashions 1862-1912. 380 Costumes from "La Mode Illustrée,"* JoAnne Olian, ed. Mineola, NY: Dover Publications, Inc., 1994; pages 30, 72, 76, 114: W. Don Smith; page 32: Reprinted from *The Gibson Girl and Her America: The Best Drawings of Charles Dana Gibson.* Edmund Gillon, ed. Mineola, NY: Dover Publications, Inc., 1969; page 37, bottom: Courtesy of Ninfa Collica; page 40, right: Broad Studio/Courtesy of Thomas Gorman; page 42, left: Courtesy of Mel Odom; pages 47, 50, 51, 60, 61,77, 89: Storm Photo; page 52, 62, 81: BARBIE and associated trademarks are owned by and used with the permission of Mattel, Inc. ©2000 Mattel, Inc. All rights reserved; page 52: Reproduction of Vera Wang's fashion sketch sold with Vera Wang Barbie doll; author's collection; pages 56, 57: Don B. Cely; page 63: Courtesy of Laura Ashley, USA. Doll manufactured by Mattel, Inc., and used with permission. pages 66, 147: Richard Creager; page 67, bottom: ©Gray Studios, Floral Park, NY/Courtesy of Grace and Jim Azzara; page 73, inset: John F. Kennedy Library, photo no. PC 2211; page 76, inset: Eugene Clay/Courtesy of Annie Wahl; page 78: Fotocolor/Courtesy of Mr. and Mrs. Franck Fonteneau; page 82: McHarg-Avon Studio/Courtesy of Anne Myatt; page 83: Mel Reingold/Reingold Photographers; page 86: H. Slawek Studio/Courtesy of Anna Petro; page 88, right: Robert K. Newsom/Park Lane Wedding Center, Ozone Park, NY/Courtesy of Ninfa Collica; pages 91, 138: Al Mida; page 94: Courtesy of Krystyna Poray Goddu; page 96: Larchmont Photography; page 98: Toni Frissel/John F. Kennedy Library; page 100, left: Library of Congress, LC-USZ6-1819; page 100, right: Library of Congress, LC-USZ62-5946; page 102: ©Wally McNamee/CORBIS; page 104: FATHER OF THE BRIDE and all related characters and elements are trademarks of Turner Entertainment Co. ©2001. Doll manufactured by Mattel, Inc., and used with permission. page 105, inset: ©Bettmann/CORBIS; pages 106, left and 107, full page: Doll manufactured by Mattel, Inc., and used with permission; page 106, right: ©2000 ABC, Inc./Ann Limongello; page 107, inset: John Paschal/Courtesy of *Days of Our Lives;* page 109, inset: Courtesy of Brynn Riordan; pages 110, 118: Al Sundstrom; page 111: Reprinted with the permission of Simon & Schuster Books for Young Readers, an imprint of Simon & Schuster Children's Publishing Division from HITTY by Rachel Field, illustrated by Dorothy P. Lathrop. Copyright 1929 Macmillan Publishing Company; copyright renewed (c) 1957 Arthur S. Pederson; pages 112, 113: Lisa Lichtenfels; page 117: Stretch Tuemmler/Courtesy of Ashton-Drake Galleries; page 122: Courtesy of Nancy Wiley; page 123: Robert O'Brien; pages 124, 125: Tamas Kish; page 132: BARBIE and associated trademarks are owned by and used with the permission of Mattel, Inc. ©2000 Mattel, Inc. All rights reserved. ©2000 Bob Mackie Design Group, Ltd. All rights reserved. page 140: ©Alison Wright/CORBIS; page 142: Philip Heath; page 143: Harold Ligtvoet; page 144: William Piltzer; page 145: Courtesy of Estelle Johnston; page 146: Courtesy of Gordon D. Gibson, Emeritus Curator of African Anthropology, Smithsonian Institution; page 148: Courtesy of Kyoko Nakanishi and Rie and Hideki Ishii.

We regret that we were unable to locate all of the photographers whose work appears in this volume, and therefore could not credit these images in full.